PENGUIN BOOKS

FEARLESS FREEDOM

Kavita Krishnan is a communist feminist activist. She is a politburo member of the CPI(ML) Liberation, and secretary of the All India Progressive Women's Association (AIPWA).

ADVANCE PRAISE FOR THE BOOK

'A book that serves up a whopper dose of truth, in an eminently readable style. Uncompromisingly feminist, what this book says about India, women, violence, control and autonomy—in private, pubic, social and political spaces—will touch a nerve in everyone. It walks the reader through real stories that made headlines, exposing the social subterfuge that masquerades as conventional wisdom, to tell us why, for our collective futures, there is no choice but to radically transform the way society understands women's freedom'—Farah Naqvi, gender and minority rights activist and author

'Kavita Krishnan gives us a chilling, unflinching account of what it means to be a woman in India. Through numerous stories of violence against women and the unbridled courage with which they continue to resist and fight back, Kavita analyses the ugly social norms that masquerade as culture. If this book does not force us to reimagine our oppressive patriarchal society, nothing will'—T.M. Krishna, author and social reform activist

'Like her essays and speeches, Kavita Krishnan's book is steeped in compassion and courage, bolstered by extensive research. Even when you disagree with her, you cannot doubt her commitment to her words. *Fearless Freedom* is a timely reminder that all oppressive systems feed off each other, and especially off the subjugation of women. It is a sharp, passionately argued critique of patriarchy in contemporary India, written in an easily readable style'—Anna M.M. Vetticad, Indian journalist and film critic

FEARLESS FREEDOM

Kavita Krishnan

PENGUIN BOOKS

An imprint of Penguin Random House

PENGUIN BOOKS

USA | Canada | UK | Ireland | Australia
New Zealand | India | South Africa | China | Singapore

Penguin Books is part of the Penguin Random House group of companies
whose addresses can be found at global.penguinrandomhouse.com

Published by Penguin Random House India Pvt. Ltd
4th Floor, Capital Tower 1, MG Road,
Gurugram 122 002, Haryana, India

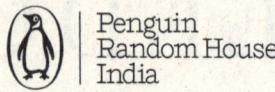

First published in Penguin Books by Penguin Random House India 2020

ISBN 9780143444688

Typeset in Adobe Caslon Pro by Manipal Technologies Limited, Manipal
Printed at Repro India Limited

www.penguin.co.in

This is a legitimate digitally printed version of the book and therefore might not
have certain extra finishing on the cover.

For Daddy
How I wish you could hold this book in your hands

CONTENTS

INTRODUCTION

If You Want to Be Safe, Why Do You Demand Freedom?

In October 2017, when women students at the Banaras Hindu University (BHU) demanded safety and freedom from the discriminatory rules that apply to the women's hostel, the then vice chancellor, Girish Chandra Tripathi, said that, after all, it was girls who got raped, not boys, and so 'girls require more security than boys'. By demanding freedom to 'roam', he said, 'girls first put themselves in danger and then start complaining'.[1] Tripathi knew his framing of the issue would resonate with the widely held common sense in India, which accepts the notion that it is more important for women to be safe than to be free; and that freedom invites danger. 'If you want to be safe, why do you demand freedom?' is a familiar question faced by Indian women.

What Tripathi underestimated, however, is the determination of young women students of BHU, and women all over India, whose movements have been striving to create a new common sense that refuses to separate the goals of 'safety' and 'freedom' for women.

On 19 December 2012, just days after the woman we now know as Jyoti Singh was gang-raped on a Delhi bus and left to die, we were demonstrating at the then Delhi chief minister Sheila Dikshit's house. There were angry young women around us, holding handmade placards that said, 'We live in a society that teaches women not to get raped instead of teaching men not to rape.' A journalist came up to me just then and asked, 'Some politicians and police officers are advising women not to go out at night as a precaution. But some women, such as nurses and journalists, *have* to work at night—what are they supposed to do?' Something about the question made me feel a red-hot, searing rage—and in my mind, its flames illuminated the problem with stark clarity. Here we were, again, asking *women* for alibis and defensive explanations and justifications for their movements, their timings, their clothes, instead of holding rapists accountable for *their* conduct and *their* disrespect for women's sovereign ownership of their own bodies.

In a speech I made a few minutes after I was asked that question, I said:

Why should women provide justifications if they want to walk out on streets alone, even if it is late at night? Why do we need reasons such as 'she has to work late' or 'she was coming home from a BPO job or a media job' to bolster such decisions? Is it a crime for women to want to go out at night, buy a cigarette or go for a walk? We do not want to hear the defensive argument that women only leave their homes to go to work . . .

We believe that regardless of whether she is indoors
or outdoors, whether it is day or night, for whatever
reason, whatever she is wearing, a woman has a right to
freedom. And it is that fearless freedom that we need to
save and protect, that we need to safeguard. The word
'safety' is overused and tired. Each of us women knows
what 'safety' means, we hear it from our parents, from
our hostel wardens, from our communities. It means
that as a woman, you must behave yourself. You should
stay at home, not dress in a particular manner, it means
that you're safe if you don't live with freedom! A huge
pile of patriarchal laws and institutions are served up
to us as 'safety' and we reject this plate of protection.
We don't want it . . . Whenever anybody speaks of
women's safety—the government machinery, the police,
the judiciary, the political parties (barring the women's
movement and the left movement)—they're talking of a
patriarchal definition of 'safety' and 'protection'. They're
not talking of protecting or defending women's fearless,
unqualified freedom. We need to tell them: if you want
to 'protect' anything, protect our fearless freedom, our
bekhauf azaadi!

In that speech I had also asked if advertisement campaigns
by governments against sexual violence, which asked men
to be 'real men' and 'protect their sisters', were really a
solution, or part of the problem. I asked how it was helpful
to ask men to be manly and brotherly towards women,
when society saw violence by brothers against sisters as
'honourable', 'manly' and 'brotherly'?

A friend and comrade, Vijay, had videotaped and uploaded the speeches made at that protest. And in the next couple of days, I slowly woke up to the fact that my speech had gone viral. The messages from unknown women, and several men, flooding my Facebook inbox showed me that the speech had touched a chord with many. I realized that what I had said about 'safety' was felt very deeply by many—and that these people were frustrated at the fact that their concerns were made to 'disappear' in the dominant discourse around women's rights, which coded 'women's safety' as curtailment of women's mobility and autonomy, confinement of women to homes or hostels, and subjection of women to a relentless regime of surveillance and control.

In the years since 2012, movements asserting women's rights to autonomy and questioning the packaging of restrictions on autonomy as 'women's safety' have grown, especially among women students and young women in cities and towns. At the same time, the organized ideological and physical offensive against women's autonomy has grown bolder, basking in political approval and patronage. This aggressive patriarchal politics threatens, over and over, to submerge and overwhelm the issue of women's autonomy, to drown out or discredit the voices of women asserting and demanding autonomy.

In our minds, in India, violent attacks on women's autonomy tend to hide in plain sight, shaped by the social structures we inhabit, our own minds supplying the disguise for them, helping them seem like harmless and innocuous ways to 'keep women safe'. Violence against women's autonomy, seen through the coloured lenses of our minds, looks like 'our culture', or like 'protection from violence'. Such violence looks normal, homely, acceptable and even protective of women.

This book is an invitation to take off the lenses and disguises, and take a fresh look at the familiar, intimate ways in which households, communities, cultures, the state and the economy work together to rationalize, and even celebrate, the curtailment of women's autonomy.

A statutory warning: the process of re-examining and challenging our comfort zones is injurious to close-mindedness, complacency and false pride. But our ability and will to change ourselves and our societies for the better is perhaps our best feature as human beings.

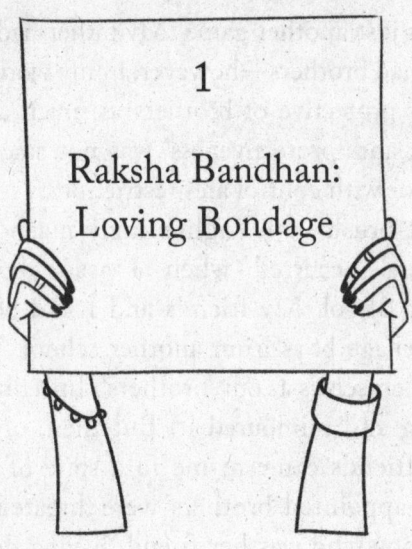

1

Raksha Bandhan:
Loving Bondage

Raksha Bandhan—or rakhi, as it is commonly known—is the festival celebrating the bond between brothers and sisters. But the very name signals the way in which our society views that relationship.

From childhood, we are taught that this is the occasion for sisters to tie the 'rakhi' (the 'raksha bandhan', or the thread/bond of protection) around the wrists of their brothers to remind them of their duty of protecting them.

My sister and I had no brothers. But I grew up tying rakhis on the wrists of a couple of boys who were close friends. The rakhis were pretty and I liked to have one of my own, so it became our habit to have the boys tie rakhis to us as well. In our families, no one spoke much about the boys' duty to protect us girls: we were friends and playmates,

1

and this was just another game. My father had sisters and my mother had brothers—however, in my world, I saw the sisters being protective of brothers as much as the other way around; and 'protectiveness' was not associated with masculinity or with control and restrictions.

My first brush with frighteningly macho 'brotherly protectiveness' occurred when I was about sixteen and in high school. My friends and I had befriended a bunch of teenage boys from another school. These boys appointed themselves as our 'brothers'. Initially, we found this amusing and humoured it. But then, one day, one of my best friends came to me in a state of panic. She said the self-appointed 'brothers' were threatening to beat up another boy who was her friend, having decided that he wasn't a suitable friend for her to have! I had trouble accepting that this kind of role-playing existed outside of Hindi movies—but it did fall to me, eventually, to let the 'brothers' know they had no business being our keepers. It was my first experience of realizing that 'brothers' were schooled in our society to police their sisters—that's what teenage boys thought 'being a brother' to a girl meant. I made a private resolve never to allow any boy to appoint himself my 'brother' again, and decided I was doing very well for myself without any brothers!

We may take Raksha Bandhan as a metaphor for the controlling familial embrace of women: for the fact that loving and 'protective' family bonds are also coercive and violent towards women. Bandhan in Hindi means 'bond' but also 'bondage'—and this, in a nutshell, expresses the contradiction at the heart of Indian families. Loving bonds are also constricting and constraining, and women struggle with the question of how to keep the love and also break the shackling bonds. Raksha Bandhan is not just a ritual or a festival—it is a living symbol of the ideology of guardianship, which refuses to respect women's autonomy. This ideology expects adult women in universities and hostels to name their 'guardians'—whether they are parents, brothers, husbands or other persons approved as guardians by the parents.

'Haven' of the Home?

> To be born a woman has been to be born, within an allotted and confined space, into the keeping of men. The social presence of women has developed as a result of their ingenuity in living under such tutelage within such a limited space.
>
> —John Berger, *Ways of Seeing*[1]

One of the most widely held beliefs is that the home is a 'haven' for girls and women, that the risks and violence lurk in wait *outside* the home, that women can be safe as long as they leave home only 'when needed'.

In February 2017, former Andhra Pradesh speaker Kodela Shiva Prasad of the Telugu Desam Party addressed a press conference ahead of a 'National Women's Parliament' hosted at Amaravati. He said, helpfully, that women were safe as long as they were parked at home like cars.

Let's say you buy a vehicle. When it is parked in the garage at home, accidents can be avoided, right? When it is taken to a bazaar or to the road, accidents are likely to happen . . . Similarly, in older times, when women were housewives, they were safe from all kinds of atrocities, except discrimination. Today, they are studying, working, and doing business. They are exposed to the society. When they are exposed to the society, they are more prone to eve-teasing, harassment, atrocities, rape and kidnap. Is it not? If they do not leave home, it doesn't happen.[2]

Shiva Prasad's analogy might be especially ridiculous and crude, however, every woman has probably heard milder, less obviously outrageous versions of the same idea. The facts, of course, belie these notions. A Delhi High Court bench, commenting on the large number of murders of women in their matrimonial homes, with the husband as the prime accused, said, 'It appears that the married women in India are safer on the streets than in their matrimonial homes.'[3] This is true, though you wouldn't know it for the disproportionate focus on stranger rapes in the media. Nor is this situation unique to India, with its 'tradition' of dowry extortion and dowry killings.

In 2012, Jyoti Singh was gang-raped and killed on a Delhi bus, and stranger rape dominated conversations about gender violence in India and the world. The same year, a United Nations study showed that of all women who were the victims of homicide globally, almost half were killed by intimate partners or family members, compared to less than 6 per cent of men killed similarly.[4] A study in Ireland found that 87 per cent of women who were murdered in Ireland over the last twenty years were killed by a man they knew; and 63 per cent were killed in their own homes.[5] The world over, then, streets are safer than their own homes for women, and homes are the places where women face the most dangerous violence, at the hands of those they know intimately. In India, however, confinement to the home itself is a form of violence that is not even acknowledged.

Prison Walls at Home

In his Hindi poem, 'Band Khidkiyon Se Takra Kar' (Crashing against Closed Windows), Gorakh Pandey, a revolutionary poet, strips away the many layers of pompous chants about women's 'greatness' to point out the obvious: the fact that women are imprisoned in the four walls of their homes—and the locked walls and windows make the home a suffocating prison, not a haven, for women.

घर-घर में दीवारें हैं
दीवारों में बंद खिड़कियाँ हैं
बंद खिड़कियों से टकराकर अपना सर
लहूलुहान गिर पड़ी है वह

नई बहू है, घर की लक्ष्मी है
इनके सपनों की रानी है
कुल की इज़्ज़त है
आधी दुनिया है
जहाँ अर्चना होती उसकी
वहाँ देवता रमते हैं
वह सीता है, सावित्री है
वह जननी है
स्वर्गादपि गरीयसी है

लेकिन बंद खिड़कियों से टकराकर
अपना सर
लहूलुहान गिर पड़ी है वह

कानूनन समान है
वह स्वतंत्र भी है
बड़े-बड़ों की नज़रों में तो
धन का एक यन्त्र भी है
भूल रहे हैं वे
सबके ऊपर वह मनुष्य है

उसे चाहिए प्यार
चाहिए खुली हवा
लेकिन बंद खिड़कियों से टकराकर
अपना सर
लहूलुहान गिर पड़ी है वह

In every home there are walls
Walls with barred windows,
Crashing against the closed windows
Bloodstained, she falls.

New bride, 'Lakshmi' of our home
Queen of his dreams
Honour of the community
Half the world
Where she's worshipped, the gods roam
She's Sita, Savitri
She's mother
She's motherland, greater than heaven

But crashing against the walls
Her head bloody
She falls.

In the eyes of the law
She's an equal
She's even free
In the eyes of great people
She's even a means of wealth
They forget
Above all she's human.

She needs love
She needs fresh air
But crashing against the closed windows
Her head bloody
She falls.

चाह रही है वह जीना
लेकिन घुट-घुट कर मरना भी
क्या जीना?

घर-घर में श्मशान-घाट है
घर-घर में फाँसी-घर है
घर-घर में दीवारें हैं
दीवारों से टकराकर
गिरती है वह

गिरती है आधी दुनिया
सारी मनुष्यता गिरती है

हम जो जिंदा हैं
हम सब अपराधी हैं
हम दण्डित हैं ।

She wants to live
But what kind of life is it,
To have to fight to breathe free?

In every home are funeral pyres
In every home the gallows loom
In every home are prison walls
Crashing against the walls
She falls.

Half the world falls
All humanity falls.

We who are alive
We are all guilty
We are all condemned.[6]

Custodial Confinement

Is it an exaggeration to speak of women's homes as prisons, to use the word 'custody' to describe them as being in 'judicial custody' or 'police custody'? Aren't most homes cherished by women as a place of privacy, safety and comfort?

To answer that question, let us take a look at some of the stark facts about Indian women's lives in their homes. The latest National Family Health Survey 2015–16 (NFHS-4) found that just 41 per cent of Indian women aged between fifteen and forty-nine are allowed to go alone to the market, to the health centre, and outside the community (NFHS-4, Table 15.13); 26 per cent of women and 16 per cent of men thought that a man would be justified in beating his wife if she went out of the house without telling him (NFHS-4, tables 15.14.1 and 15.14.2).

Do women from Dalit and Adivasi communities have greater freedom of movement than women of the dominant castes? The NFHS-4 findings don't support this widely held belief: there is very little variation amongst women of Scheduled Castes, Scheduled Tribes, Other Backward Classes and 'other' castes when it comes to being allowed to go out of the house.

Another study, the India Human Development Survey (IHDS), made a distinction between women being able to go out alone and women having to seek permission to go out, finding that:

[B]etter educated women make more decisions in the household and are able to go to more places on their own; however, there is less evidence that they can go without asking for permission from someone in the household. Similarly, women working for pay or working in a family business can make more household decisions and can go to more places on their own, but again there is no significant relationship with whether they can go out without taking permission to do so.

The IHDS also found that:

[T]here are surprisingly few differences among women in different social groups. Dalit and OBC women do have more freedom to leave the household by themselves, though surprisingly, this freedom of movement does not extend to Adivasi women. There are no measurable differences between Hindu, Muslim and women of other religious minority communities. Also, caste differences are not found in the case of the more private household empowerment measures of decision-making and women having to ask permission to leave the house.[7]

The NFHS-4 found that young and never-married women were subjected to the greatest restrictions on movement: older, married women gained more freedom of movement, but still, just 55 per cent of women between the ages of forty and forty-nine enjoyed such freedom. It's likely that the restrictions on women loosen as they age, because the burden of their household labour is likely to have shifted in good measure to a younger woman—a daughter or a daughter-in-law, who is also the subject of intense surveillance and control.

If you think education makes for greater freedom for women, you are wrong. Education contributes only marginally to freedom of movement: 42.9 per cent women with no schooling and 45.3 per cent women with twelve years or more of schooling have freedom of movement (NFHS-4).

What do these facts and figures really mean?

They translate to a life lived 'crashing against walls', like a bird caught in a closed room, battered by every attempt to escape and fly free.

There's really no way to dress up this life and romanticize it as 'safe', as the only life where one's 'honour' is safe.

It means that young girls and women grow up under almost-total surveillance, denied even the mere dream of privacy. It means that newly-wed brides are even more confined when they are married into faraway homes: like migrant labour just arrived in the city, they are isolated, unable to draw on their friends and familiar neighbourhoods.

This does not mean that these violent homes are not 'loving' homes: the point is that love, concern and caring do not automatically translate into respect for autonomy and personhood. The love is for the *idea* of the daughter or sister or daughter-in-law—and that love may turn into violence if the woman and her choices fall foul of the *idea* of what she is expected to be.

Such intense and obsessive confinement of women is not 'safety'. It's time we recognized it as violence in its own right. The cautionary tale of the 'Lakshman *rekha*' distracts us with the fear of the evil Ravana lurking in wait if women breach the 'circle of safety' at their doorstep. It makes us forget that to be confined within four walls is to be prevented from living life fully, to be condemned to the suffocating existence of a caged bird.

Violence against Women's Autonomy: Disguised as 'Rape'

The everyday violence against women's autonomy becomes most acute when young women fall in love in violation of the Lakshman rekha fault lines of caste and faith. We hear of these crimes only when the woman and/or her lover/husband are killed and the media describes it as an 'honour killing'. But the fact is that such violence is acute even when it stops short of a killing. Such killings take place when other forms of violence intended to prevent such relationships and marriages fail. There is no available public record of such violence. But it hides in plain sight—and one way to spot it is to take a close look at rape-case statistics.

In 2014, *The Hindu* tracked 583 rape cases decided by New Delhi's district trial courts in 2013. Its findings were startling: over 40 per cent of 'what is classified as rape (in Delhi Police files) is actually parental criminalization of consensual sexual relationships, often when it comes to inter-caste and inter-religious couples'.[8]

Take a moment to absorb that fact. Let me break it down for you. Rape is a sexual act committed in violation of a woman's consent: the only basis for a rape case involving an adult woman has to be that she says she was subjected to a sexual act without her consent. When an adult woman's parents file complaints of rape, the police should not register a case of rape. When the matter is one of love between two teenagers of similar age, too, women's groups strongly express the opinion that such relationships should not be classified as statutory rape, even if one or both are below the age of eighteen. They argue strongly that a distinction needs to be made between a much older adult having a sexual relationship with a minor girl between the ages of fifteen and eighteen (such cases ought to qualify as statutory rape), and love relationships between two teenagers without much age gap. But the Parliament in 2013 caved to a media-orchestrated moral storm and *raised* the age of consent from sixteen to eighteen, thus automatically criminalizing young love and branding all young love as 'rape'. In a society where inter-caste and interfaith friendships and love face violent opposition, the age of consent as defined in the rape law now strengthens the hands of the patriarchs who brand 'love' as 'rape'. To make the point even more clear, let's recognize that parents who may be eager and willing to get their daughters, aged between fifteen and eighteen, married to boys of *their* choice (that is a boy from an approved caste and community) in violation of the law that prohibits child marriage, will accuse a boy *their daughter loves of her own choice* of being a rapist. How can the law refuse to make a distinction between the two instances?

The violence faced by the girls and women in these cases is not 'rape'—it is violence that remains unnamed, unrecognized and can even pass off as 'rescuing our daughter from rape'. *The Hindu* described the violence behind these 'rape' statistics:

> In two-thirds of the cases, the supposed 'victim' girl or woman 'deposed consistently before the police, doctors, magistrate, district judge and under cross-examination that she had eloped and had sexual relations—and in most cases got married and sometimes had children—with

the accused because she was in love with him'. In all these cases, 'girls depose about the suffering they faced at the hands of their parents—beatings, confinement, threats, being forced to undergo medical examinations, abortions—even as they plead before the court they be allowed to stay with their husbands. A large number involved inter-caste and inter-religious couples'.[9]

In all the remaining cases, the girl or woman 'deposed in at least one instance—either in the initial FIR, or during her medical examination, or in her statement to the magistrate—that she was in love with the accused and went away with him of her own will. However, in court she supports her parents' and the prosecution's case'.[10]

How does she change her mind? If she is kept in a shelter, she is often prevented from meeting or having any contact with her lover's or husband's family. Instead, she is allowed only to meet her own parents and family, who exert continuous pressure on her. If she is sent home, the violence inflicted on her in the custody of her parents' home—beatings, confinement, threats and forced abortions described by the girls/women in two-thirds of the cases—break their will.

The study by *The Hindu* said:

In case after case, as well as in interviews with *The Hindu*, the behaviour of the girls' parents was shocking: they arrive at the hotel the couple has eloped to and drag them home, they beat and even injure the couple (in one case breaking the girl's spine), they threaten her even with acid, they force her to submit to invasive medical tests and in many cases, even to an abortion.[11]

Unfortunately, the law—as drafted by patriarchal parliamentarians ignoring the pleas of women's movement groups based on their vast and long experience on the ground—refuses now to allow judges to make any distinction between young love and statutory rape. It has chosen to validate the violence against girls' and women's autonomy, and brand love as 'rape'. The law and the judiciary also turn a blind eye to the evidence of horrific violence meted out to women and girls in parental or community custody, and in fact offers itself as a tool to regulate and control the sexuality and autonomy of girls and women, and disguise such regulation as rescue from rape. Even in cases involving adult women, the judiciary has, on multiple occasions, betrayed that it shares the patriarchal anxieties about daughters' choices, especially when these anxieties are compounded by a growing climate of Islamophobia.

For LGBTQ persons, as for women, the parental home can easily become a prison as soon as they exercise their personhood and sexual autonomy. Very often, the judiciary and judicial systems work to discipline and punish, rather than respect and defend their autonomy and sexual orientation and gender identity. A recent study documented a case in Chennai, in which a lesbian woman was held captive inside her home by her parents. The woman's partner filed a petition asking for the woman to be produced in court. Asked by the judge if she preferred to stay at home with her parents or go with her partner, the woman clearly declared that she would like to join her partner. The judge, instead of respecting the woman's decision, referred to her as a 'person with different values', and sent her to a government-run 'shelter' home for women, to think about her decision. In the next hearing, the detention had had its effect: wishing to avoid prolonged incarceration in the 'shelter' home, the woman opted to go back to her family, and the judge promptly 'allowed' her to do so.[12]

Likewise, in Kerala, a woman was held captive by her family to prevent her from living with her partner, a transgender man. The latter approached the court, and in court the woman clearly said she wished to live with her partner. But instead of ensuring that she was free to do as she pleased, the judge replaced the parental custody and captivity with the captivity of a government-run shelter home, where she remained for a long period. Only when she refused to let the incarceration break her will and stuck to her position in repeated court appearances did the court finally agree to let her join her partner.[13]

It appears that the patriarchal ideology of guardianship is deeply entrenched even in India's judicial apparatus. Sudha Ramalingam, a human rights lawyer who has been involved in several such cases, said that in these cases, 'There is no Constitution, no law, only morality.'[14] The judges tend to uphold the dominant, patriarchal, casteist and homophobic 'morality' rather than the law and the Constitution, when it comes to the autonomy of women and LGBTQ persons.

Respect for Personhood

A woman is a person, not the property (however loved and cherished) of the family or the community. Why is this concept so hard to grasp? The clue to the answer lies in the fact that in any given society, our emotions are shaped and trained in large part by social and economic structures. We are not born expressing 'love' for our partner through bouquets of roses or jasmine flowers; or for a daughter or sister through aggression towards their boyfriend. These are 'structures of feeling' that we learn.

In India, caste underpins social, economic and emotional structures deeply. Caste—an oppressive hierarchical structure—plays a huge role in determining where we live; who our neighbours are; who our schoolmates are; who our friends are; what work we do; and, of course, who we marry. And to maintain caste, it is crucial to control women's sexuality: any expression of sexual choice by a woman poses a threat to the caste system.

Historian Uma Chakravarti writes that Brahminical patriarchy has for long regarded women of upper castes as 'gateways' into the caste system—requiring careful surveillance to preserve upper-caste purity—and this 'obsessive concern with policing female sexuality' has become a stubborn feature across caste groups, enjoying widespread approval and consent.[15] When women exercise free choice in sexual matters, writes Chakravarti, 'the whole social fabric seems to suffer a terrible tear'.[16] Choice is also infectious—a woman who chooses her own partner is also more likely to demand a share of her ancestral property, and this explains in part why the granting of legal inheritance rights to women has increased the violence against women's marriage choices in Haryana.[17]

Shaped by Brahminical patriarchy, parents and brothers learn to express 'love' for and 'duty' towards a daughter or a sister by surveilling her and controlling her movements. Sadhana Subramaniam's film *India's Forbidden Love: An Honour Killing on Trial*, which was part of the 'Witness' documentary series on Al Jazeera, focused on the trial of the parents of a woman called Kausalya for the murder of her husband, Shankar, who was hacked to death in public for being a Dalit man who married a woman from a dominant caste. Two juxtaposed scenes in this documentary say a lot. Kausalya, transformed by the brutal murder of Shankar into a crusader against caste patriarchy, is watching the news when the verdict is being announced—her father has been convicted but her mother and uncle have been acquitted. With two of the accused free, Kausalya knows that her life is in danger—they have been threatening to kill her as well. As the ticker on the TV screen reads 'mother acquitted' she turns around and says to the channel's reporter, 'Who edits your news? Tell them not to say "mother", call her by her name.' The next scene is in Kausalya's parents' home, where her mother is recalling, with a smile and obvious fondness, how Kausalya knew only how to cook dosai: 'When I was sick, she would cook dosai for me.' Her mother then says that she had warned Kausalya, 'If you betray us, fall in love and elope, I'll kill you.'

Our society, as it stands now, produces the emotions felt and expressed by Kausalya—her love for Shankar, her fierce determination to fight for social change even by risking her own life. It also produces the emotions felt by her parents: of 'shame' and 'hurt honour' and murderous violence as a way of redeeming lost social status. Which emotions will we choose to nurture and stand by: the love and courage of defiant sons and daughters, breaking the barbed-wire boundaries of caste, faith and enforced sexual orientation and heterosexuality, or what the poet Alok Dhanwa called '*kuleenta ki hinsa*' (the violence of the high-born)?[18]

Kaliyug, Caste and Disobedient Women

In the Hindu imagination, Kaliyug is the degenerate and apocalyptic modern era: a 'world turned upside down' marked by the breakdown/inversion of class, caste, gender, age and other hierarchies. In Hindi and north Indian popular culture, the modern and sexually autonomous young woman who disobeys and defies her parents and elders is the most well-recognized symbol of *ghor* Kaliyug (terrible Kaliyug).

To understand the extent to which women's sexual autonomy is seen in India as threatening to the social order, we must come to grips with the fact that caste has been—and remains—the foundation of that social order, to which women's sexual autonomy poses a great threat. Kaliyug in Hindu mythology is quite specifically an age when the caste and gender order disintegrates—and this disintegration is seen in the dominant ideology as a calamity, not a beneficial event.

The epic poem Mahabharata, for instance, has a detailed description of Kaliyug as a world turned upside down, marked by Sudras doing the work of Brahmins and vice versa, Brahmins being treated like commoners while Sudras demand and enjoy respect, Sudras refusing to serve Brahmins, disobedient women and 'mixed marriages' between castes.[19]

Arti Dhand points out that in the descriptions of Kaliyug in the Mahabharata, 'The sexual intermingling of classes is treated as the very worst state of affairs in society, the hallmark of society's descent into chaos before the final dissolution of the world.'[20] She notes that 'all descriptions of Kaliyuga include graphic representations of *varnasamkara*, the sexual corruption of classes. Distinctions between high and low are erased . . . In these grim accounts, the mixture of classes is viewed with more than just distaste. It is imbued with real horror.'[21] Dhand perceptively notes that 'the biggest single source of anxiety for the writers of the Mahabharata' involved women who married 'beneath' them. Such women were 'virulently condemned', with elaborate tortures being prescribed as punishments for Sudra men and Brahmin women who intermarried.[22]

The Bhagavad Gita—possibly the most popular religious text for modern-day Hindus—begins with Arjuna, wracked by doubt on the battlefield about the righteousness of the impending fratricidal bloodshed, painting a graphic spectre for Krishna about the lawlessness that such fratricide might usher in. And 'intermixture of caste' and the resulting breakdown of the rigid divisions of 'caste duties' (that is labour assigned according to birth and caste) are described as the very essence of such lawlessness:

Because of the ascendancy of lawlessness, Krishna,
The family women are corrupted;
When women are corrupted, O Krishna,
The intermixture of caste is born.
Intermixture brings to hell

The family destroyers and the family, too;
The ancestors of these indeed fall,
Deprived of offerings of rice and water.
By these wrongs of the family destroyers,
Producing intermixture of caste,
Caste duties are abolished,
And eternal family laws also.[23]

In this passage, women are seen to be 'corrupted' when they marry outside rather than inside the caste—resulting in what is visualized as the ultimate calamity: the mixing up of castes and the breakdown of the caste-based division of labour.

I've often come across rationalizations of caste, claiming that caste was not originally conceived as an assignment of labour based on birth into a particular caste, and was/is, instead, simply a description of different kinds of labour, that anyone could do depending on one's aptitude or wish. A recent instance of such an argument was a tweet by journalist Abhijit Majumder, which declared, 'I'm a Kshatriya when I fight and defend my rights and ideas, a Vaishya when I'm engaged in gainful work, a Sudra when I'm cleaning things, and a Brahmin by birth. Above all, I'm a Hindu and an Indian, and proudly so.'[24] This statement tries to whitewash the oppressive foundations of caste, by pretending to be innocent of the fact that persons born in oppressed castes face untouchability and apartheid, and can be killed for daring to cross caste boundaries—by voting, going to college, dressing smartly, playing loud music, and, of course, for marrying women from castes 'above' their own.

Majumder elaborated on the theme in another tweet: 'Varnas were meant to categorize work in society. Upper castes used this analysis to tie people down to castes by heredity. Then came untouchability, many believe with invaders/colonialists. We must take caste back to its original analysis, to believe every varna resides in each of us.'[25] Is, as Majumder argues, caste oppression a relatively modern distortion of a varna system that was originally a benign 'categorization of work' in conception? Was the relationship between 'caste' and 'labour' originally closer to the sense conveyed by Majumder's tweets? Is Majumder right when he implies that the oppressive aspects of caste must be blamed, not on the original Hindu concept of caste/varna but on the 'invaders' (read Muslim/Mughal rulers) and (British) colonialists? Reading Krishna's reply to Arjuna in the Gita clears up this question pretty soon.

Krishna's exposition of 'duty' to Arjuna is very explicitly based on birth-based caste. Krishna says: 'Better one's own duty though deficient than the duty of another well performed. Better is death in one's own [caste] duty . . . The duty of another [caste] invites danger.'[26] Here, 'one's own duty' (*swadharma*) and 'another's duty' (*paradharma*) are clearly defined as duties one is born to do according to the caste one is born into. It is brutally clear here that 'duty' has nothing to do with one's ability or aptitude—one must do one's caste-assigned duty even if one is deficient at it, and one must not do the work assigned to another caste even if one is very good at it. The Gita, in Krishna's voice, elaborates on this theme, leaving no room whatsoever for any comforting liberal interpretation.

Krishna declares:

> The system of four castes was created by Me,
> According to the distribution of the qualities and their
> acts.[27]

Is this divinely ordained categorization of the four castes based on work that is freely chosen according to aptitude and skill, or is it based on birth regardless of aptitude, skill or choice? The Gita is unambiguous and crystal-clear that the 'innate' qualities of persons, and the corresponding acts and duties, are all based rigidly on birth.

> The duties of the Brahmins, the Kshatriyas, the Vaishyas,
> And of the Sudras, Arjuna,
> Are distributed according to
> The qualities which arise from their
> own nature.
> Tranquility, restraint, austerity, purity,
> Forgiveness and uprightness,
> Knowledge, wisdom and faith in God
> Are the duties of the Brahmins,
> Born of their innate nature.
> Heroism, majesty, firmness, skill,
> Not fleeing in battle,
> Generosity and lordly spirit
> Are the duties of the Kshatriyas,
> Born of their innate nature.
> Plowing, cow-herding and trade
> Are the duties of the Vaishyas,

Born of their innate nature.
Service is the duty of the Sudras,
Born of their innate nature.[28]

In fact, the Gita specifically prescribes that the duties assigned on the basis of one's own birth/caste must be performed *even* if one is no good at them, and one must *never* perform the duties assigned to another caste *even if* one is capable of performing them. All the noble qualities belong to the Brahmins and the Kshatriyas—the Vaishyas are defined only in terms of their occupations rather than any fine qualities; and the Sudras are defined solely by their duty to serve (i.e. labour for) the non-Sudras.

... Better one's own duty, though imperfect,
Than the duty of another well performed;
Performing the duty prescribed by one's own nature,
One does not incur evil.
One should not abandon the duty to which one is born
Even though it be deficient, Arjuna.[29]

This passage makes it very clear that in the worldview of the Gita, a person from an oppressed caste, even if well suited to intellectual pursuits, must not abandon their work of 'service' to those of other castes and seek instead to acquire knowledge or wisdom, because to do so would be evil and dangerous. One's 'inherent nature' is based on the caste one is born into, *irrespective* of one's abilities and aptitudes.

And how is caste maintained and reproduced? By controlling women and ensuring they do not cross caste borders. Women, if allowed to roam freely across caste borders, having sexual relationships and even bearing children with men of 'lower' castes, present a terrible danger to the entire social edifice of caste. In the words of Arti Dhand, in the Mahabharata, 'Women's sexuality poses a threat to the very foundations on which society is based and is therefore singled out as a frightening and uncontrollable force, potentially beneficial to society, but potentially also destructive.'[30] So, in the Mahabharata— and, we may add, in modern-day popular culture and in widely prevalent common sense as well—'women figure as key ingredients in the breakdown of society in descriptions of the Kaliyug . . . Women contribute to the general collapse of civilization through neglect of social and familial duty. They lose reverence for the codes of behavior encouraged by *pativrat* dharma, and act in ego-indulgent, idiosyncratic ways. Hence they are critical agents in creating the distress signaled by the age and are the source of disquiet and difficulty.'[31]

In caste, thus, lies the key to understanding India's obsession with controlling and curbing women's autonomy. I am introducing this idea—of women's autonomy and the breakdown of the caste-based division of labour and labourers—as a key element of the spectre of the degenerate modern Kaliyug early on, because it is an idea that is still very much with us. We will come across the same idea in many contexts that we will discuss later in the book: in the opposition of nationalist leaders like Tilak to women's education; in the writings of Yogi Adityanath, who argues that women's power must be tightly controlled because of its potentially destructive power if allowed freedom; in the repeated, fascinated invocation by right-wing politicians of the spectre of that folk-devil: the woman student whose assertions of autonomy makes her promiscuous, roaming around on a campus which, because it creates the space for inter-caste sexual relationships, must be a den for 'free' sex. We will also, in the course of the book, meet women who welcome Kaliyug specifically for its freedoms, and whose quest for autonomy leads them to confront and resist caste.

The Four Walls of Patriarchy

Confinement to the home is the most common form of oppression and violence against women in India. The confinement is achieved through coercion (the threat, and use, of violence) but also through consent (where girls and women internalize patriarchal moral values valorizing voluntary confinement and stigmatizing free and autonomous mobility).

Such restrictions on autonomy and mobility are joined at the hip with several other—more visible and recognizable—forms of gender violence: domestic violence, honour crimes and, of course, rape culture.

The NFHS-4 findings show that a considerable proportion of not only men but women, too, believe that domestic violence is justified punishment for violating the restrictions on autonomy and failure to fulfil the obligatory forms of labour expected from women in households.

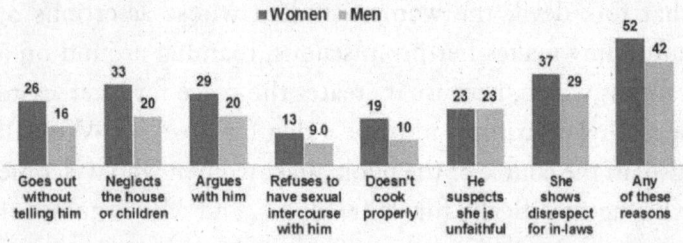

Figure 15.4 Attitudes Toward Wife Beating

Percentage of women and men age 15-49 who agree that a husband is justified in beating his wife for specific reasons

(Source: NFHS-4, Figure 15.4)

Many believe a husband is justified in beating his wife if she goes out without telling him (26 per cent women and 16 per cent men); neglects the house or children (33 per cent women and 20 per cent men); shows disrespect for in-laws (37 per cent women and 29 per cent men); or if suspected of being unfaithful (23 per cent women and men both).

The NFHS-4 also found that attitudes towards wife-beating had changed only marginally since the last NFHS round in 2005–06: 'For women, agreement with all seven reasons justifying wife-beating has declined by only 3 percentage points from 54 per cent in NFHS-3; for men, the corresponding decline is 9 percentage points, from 51 per cent in NFHS-3' (NFHS-4, p. 512). Also, 'agreement with wife-beating tends to increase with age for women but decreases with age for men' (NFHS-4, Table 15.14.1 and Table 15.14.2).

How do we make sense of the above facts? To me, with years of experience in the women's movement, it is not particularly surprising to find that a larger proportion of women as compared to men voice justifications for domestic violence. Patriarchal social relations, like other oppressive relations, do not rely on coercion alone—they rely in very large measure on being able to acquire the consent of the subordinated classes or sections of people. Younger women, especially young married women, bear the greatest proportion of the burden of household labour. Young men—and their parents—are encouraged to see themselves as entitled to the domestic services provided by a wife or a daughter-in-law. Older women, who have in their youth borne the burden of such labour, look forward to passing the burden on to daughters-in-law. Daughters-in-law are kept isolated from their parents and friends by restrictions on autonomy, expected to be subordinate to in-laws, to perform household labour and face domestic violence if they fall short in any of these areas. And unsurprisingly, it is older women who are expected to enforce the rules and supervise the labour and subordination of the daughters-in-law, even as they themselves have now earned some measure of respite from the surveillance and subordination.

So, domestic violence is closely linked to household labour, and to restrictions on autonomy and confinement to the home. 'Safety' is the pretext for confining women to homes; the outcome is to create consent for the domestic servitude of women.

We have already seen how restrictions on autonomy provide the rationale behind honour crimes, even allowing such crimes to masquerade as 'safety' for women.

Restrictions on autonomy are also inextricably linked with rape culture and victim-blaming. In a short documentary by Quint on the rape culture in Haryana, a schoolboy studying in Class VIII says, 'Both boys and girls are responsible for rape. Rapes happen because girls loiter on the streets. Girls should not leave the house unless they have some work.'[32] And he is not alone. The idea that women out in public spaces is the reason for rape is one that is widely believed and propagated, even by senior police officers.

Ironically, women all over the world, and in India too, spend a lot more time and money than men on strategies to 'stay safe'. A study by economist Girija Borker found, for instance, that woman students of Delhi University were spending much more than men on transportation and settling for colleges less desirable than the ones they qualified for, because of safety considerations.[33] Yet, women victims of sexual violence are routinely blamed for having failed to choose safety and to avoid violence! Restrictions on autonomy are part of the ecosystem that enables rape culture.

Above all, what needs to be recognized is that restrictions on autonomy *do not* achieve safety. Isolation and confinement in the house creates a culture of silence around violence inside the home. And those women who are 'allowed out to study' constantly fear an enforced return to the confines of the parental home, and so they're afraid of complaining of sexual harassment or rape, lest the parents get to know. Girls and women do love their freedom to study, to have friends, to have a job; however much they hate sexual harassment and violence, they do not want to risk those freedoms as the cost of complaining.

Jitender Chattar, a farmer from Haryana, was once notorious as the leader who claimed 'chow mein causes rape'. But to his credit, he didn't cling lifelong to such misogynist myths. In a recent article about his support for his wife's quest for justice against gang rape, he made the insightful observation that schoolgirls facing rampant sexual harassment 'would never complain to their parents as it could mean no longer being allowed to go to school to study'—a valid apprehension because 'families had forced their girls to drop out of college' because of sexual harassment.[34]

I have worked with survivors of sexual harassment and violence for the past two decades, and, in my experience, the number one reason why women students prefer not to make formal complaints about violence is their fear that when their parents get to know, their education will be curtailed and they will be made to 'return home' and get married. Loving, caring parents need to think—why does your daughters' fear that you will curtail their already limited freedom override their urge for justice when they experience sexual violence?

Want your daughters 'safe'? Let them know—early— that you have their back; that they and *their freedom* have your unconditional support; that they will not be blamed or pay with the loss of their freedom for sexual violence. That will embolden them to speak up about sexual harassment and violence rather than suffer in silence.

'Safety' for women cannot lie in keeping them within the four walls of patriarchy. Restrictions on women's autonomy are the stuff of which the four walls of patriarchy are made—they enable all other forms of gender discrimination and violence. Addressing these other forms of violence without tackling the attacks on autonomy is like rearranging the furniture in the patriarchal house. Bring down the walls instead, and the whole patriarchal edifice will come tumbling down.

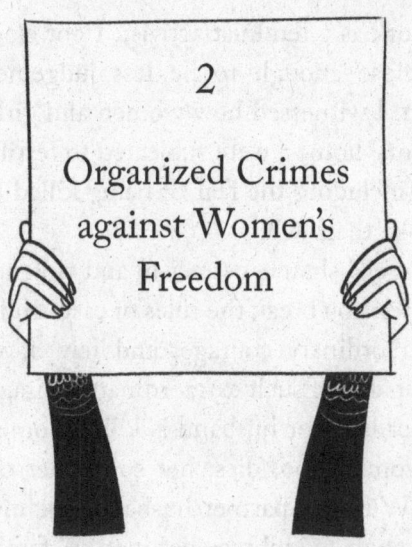

2

Organized Crimes against Women's Freedom

Women exercise great courage when they fall in love or marry in defiance of their parents. Why does that courage—and even that love—seem to evaporate if their parents/communities manage to eliminate the lover/husband, or get them back into their custody? Growing up, and as a college student, I used to puzzle over this every time I read news stories about women defending their family members who had killed their partners in the name of 'honour'. If you loved someone deeply enough for you to take immense emotional, financial and physical risks to be with him, why would you turn loyal to his killers (your parents/family members)? Why would you, in a police station, declare that he is your rapist, not your lover?

In my work as a feminist activist, I got closer to these situations—close enough to be less judgemental about these women. I witnessed how women and girls, confined in their parents' homes, were subjected to terrible cruelties and torture (including the fear of being killed by kith and kin) that broke their will.

Risking social shame, ostracism and violence, which is inevitable when you break the rules of caste and patriarchy, calls for extraordinary courage, and few of us ordinary people are capable of such extraordinary courage.

When her lover or husband is killed, some vital spark inside the woman, too, dies: her spirit, her courage, her confidence. With her partner/husband, she may have felt confident enough to embrace her in-laws' family and seek love there—but without him, she loses that confidence. Her bid for independence and her attempt at rebellion foiled, she thinks she can survive only by reconciling herself to her parents, brothers and community.

It's hard enough standing up to one's parents and brothers and other loved ones when they are all bearing down upon you to give up your wish to love or marry who you like. But when family pressures are backed up by organized violence and political pressure, young couples and ordinary young women who lack access to any women's movement find the situation overwhelmingly daunting.

The Caste Councils

Violence by the caste councils (called khap panchayats or katta panchayats) against inter-caste and same-*gotra* couples is probably the best-recognized form of organized violence against women's autonomy. The khaps are known to order the murders of inter-caste (especially relationships in which a Dalit man marries a Jat woman) and same-gotra couples. In March 2018, a Supreme Court ruling holding khap interference in consensual marriages 'absolutely illegal', observed that the khap 'behaves like a patriarchal monarch which treats the wives, sisters and daughters as subordinate, even servile or self-sacrificing, persons . . . having no individual autonomy, desire and identity'. The Supreme Court also noted that the perception of so-called 'honour' as defined by these caste panchayats was nothing but 'a sense of masculine dominance'.[1] The Supreme Court rejected arguments made by the Manushi Sangathan that attempted to clear the khap panchayats of the taint of honour crimes and killings. The judgment, however, is not an indictment of khap panchayats or of 'honour killings' alone, but of any curtailment of women's autonomy and privacy by anyone, including, of course, family members: '[Any] kind of torture or torment or ill-treatment in the name of honour that tantamounts [sic] to atrophy of choice of an individual relating to love and marriage by any assembly, whatsoever nomenclature it assumes, is illegal and cannot be allowed a moment of existence.'

The story of Manoj and Babli exposes any claims by organizations like the Manushi Sangathan that the khap panchayats are benign community councils that may oppose *sagotra* (same gotra) marriages but do not order, approve or propagate violence against such marriages.

In April 2007, a young couple in Karora village, Kaithal, in Haryana, got married. Twenty-three-year-old Manoj and nineteen-year-old Babli had fallen in love. Knowing that Babli's parents would object to the marriage because both were from the same gotra, they eloped. Babli's family filed an FIR, accusing Manoj and his family of kidnapping Babli. Manoj and Babli appeared in Kaithal court and said that their relationship was consensual and that they were married. The court ordered the superintendent of police, Kaithal, 'to ensure the safety of lives of Manoj and Babli'. Accompanied by five policemen, Manoj and Babli left Kaithal for Chandigarh. But the policemen abandoned them at Pipli (Kurukshetra). At least one of the policemen informed Babli's family members exactly where to find the couple. Three men from their village stopped the bus they were in and forced the couple to deboard. They kidnapped the couple and took them away. Babli's brother forced her to consume poison and watch her uncle strangle Manoj to death. The bodies of Manoj and Babli were thrown into a canal and found much later. When Manoj's mother, Chanderpati, and his sister, Seema, pursued justice for the couple, they were first offered bribes to take back the case. When they refused, they received threats to themselves and their dependants. They, however, displayed great courage and refused to back down. The Banwala khap then imposed an economic and social boycott on them. Gangaraj, the leader of the Banwala khap and a prominent local leader of the Congress party, justified the boycott, saying, 'The key reasons for the boycott are, firstly, we lost our girl, and the false charge filed against us and the girl's family by the groom's mother . . . Anyone who talks to them or trades anything with them will be fined Rs 25,000 and that person will be boycotted as well.'[2]

The Banwala khap leaders organized a murder attempt on Seema too. The police continued to display its bias in favour of the accused Gangaraj. The Banwala khap also announced its intention to repeat the Manoj–Babli killing with another couple, Vedpal and Sonia, saying, 'If disgraceful acts like these occur, then such incidents will obviously be repeated.' Soon after, Vedpal was murdered.

A sessions court convicted the accused in the Manoj–Babli case, offering some hope to those resisting the khaps in Haryana. The Punjab and Haryana High Court later acquitted the main accused, Gangaraj, and another convict, Satish, while commuting the death sentence that the sessions court had awarded to Babli's brother and her uncles. Seema and Chanderpati continue to try to secure a conviction for Gangaraj in the Supreme Court.

Babli, Manoj, Seema and Chanderpati refused to succumb to the threats, violence and boycotts imposed by the khaps. Babli and Manoj were killed for this, Seema survived murderous attacks and both Chanderpati, a widow, and Seema continue to fight and stand tall.[3]

But for every Babli, every Seema, every Chanderpati, there are many women and girls whom the khaps succeed in intimidating and torturing into submission. Those are the stories we do not hear, because its survivors have been successfully muzzled.

Political Appeasement of Khaps

In India's political discourse, the right wing has successfully associated the word 'appeasement' with any policies that recognize and seek to correct caste and religious inequalities and discrimination. When the oppressed or marginalized (the Dalits or Muslim minorities) make their presence felt in politics, they are labelled a 'vote-bank'. But the political attempts to consolidate dominant castes and communities around the most regressive ideas and institutions are never called 'appeasement' or 'vote-bank politics'.

The support for khap panchayats across the political spectrum is one of the most glaring instances of appeasement of violent and regressive institutions. As we saw in the murders of Manoj, Babli and Vedpal, khap panchayats openly boast of their intention to kill couples who defy their diktats, carry out those killings, and then use social and economic boycotts to deter those who seek justice. These tactics are not limited to honour crimes. In 2010, two Dalits were burnt alive and the homes of eighteen Dalits burnt down in Mirchpur, Haryana.[4] After the carnage, threats from the khap panchayats of dominant Jat communities forced 150 Dalit families to flee the village.[5] As many as twelve khap panchayats held an eleven-day agitation against any move to arrest and prosecute those responsible for the Mirchpur carnage.[6]

Yet, despite all the undeniable evidence of khap panchayats' involvement in violence against women, couples and Dalits, there is considerable political support for them.

The political defence of khaps takes two forms: one, to argue that khaps are basically benign community organizations doing valuable welfare and dispute-resolution work, with nothing to tie them to honour crimes; and two, to actively support the khaps' regressive demands such as banning sagotra relationships and outlawing the right of daughters to inherit ancestral property.

Bharatiya Janata Party (BJP) leader Manohar Lal Khattar (now Haryana's chief minister) justified khap diktats against sagotra marriages, saying in October 2014, 'Khaps maintain the tradition of a girl and boy being brother and sister. They are just making sure that a girl and boy do not see each other in the wrong way. These rulings help prevent rapes too.'[7]

Just one year before Khattar's statement, the then Haryana chief minister Bhupinder Singh Hooda from the Congress party, said khap panchayats didn't order 'honour killings', only girls' parents did, advocating a change of mindset rather than action against the khaps. He also indicated that the khaps' objection to sagotra marriages was justified, asking the reporter, 'Tell me one thing: how many of you marry within the gotra. I am asking, do you marry within your gotras?'[8] Hooda also compared khaps to non-governmental organizations (NGOs) and resident welfare associations (RWAs).[9]

Both the Texas-educated businessman and then Congress member of parliament (MP) Naveen Jindal, and the Indian National Lok Dal leader Om Prakash Chautala have supported the khap demand to ban sagotra marriages.[10]

And it's not only BJP and Congress leaders. Aam Aadmi Party convenor and Delhi chief minister Arvind Kejriwal, in his book *Swaraj*, makes the point that empowered gram sabhas need not turn into dictatorial khap panchayats. That point is fair enough—but he specifically expresses ambiguity on the khaps' involvement in honour crimes, writing, 'Whether khap panchayats had given such orders [to kill couples] or not is a debatable issue.'[11] When we see khap leaders openly giving statements in newspapers and to TV channels threatening sagotra couples with murder, is their role in such killings still 'debatable'? Remember, Vedpal of Kaithal was killed after a leader of the Banwala khap openly said in a video-taped interview that he would be killed.

A more sophisticated defence of khap panchayats has been offered by noted social scientist and leader of the Swaraj India party Yogendra Yadav. In a Facebook post on 31 January 2014 (he was at the time spokesperson of the Aam Aadmi Party), he wrote:

> Every community [caste, tribe, ethnic group] has its internal mechanisms for routine dispute resolution. Such communitarian systems are not only permissible but are healthy and indeed essential. Pushing any and every social dispute into courts of law is unhealthy, unaffordable and socially destructive. If this is what khap panchayats do and to the extent to which they do this, there is nothing wrong with khap panchayats or any other caste/community association. The trouble begins when this dispute resolution becomes coercive and violates the law of the land.[12]

In an interview, he said, '[If] they [khaps] try to resolve disputes by listening to only one community or by coercion, then we as a party do not accept that . . . All castes and communities have social organizations for internal dispute-resolution but no coercion can be permitted. The law of the land is supreme and a murder is a murder.'[13]

But Yadav's argument is disingenuous and misleading. When a body is allowed to 'represent' a community, without taking special pains to overturn the caste, gender and other hierarchies that already exist within that community, it is bound to reflect and perpetuate those hierarchies. Moreover, khaps exercise power outside their communities too.

Khaps seek to maintain the dominance of the Jats. They claim to speak for the 'entire community', but Dalits and women have no place within the khaps. Can institutions controlled by dominant-caste men be allowed the right to resolve 'social disputes' in a democracy, and can such a manner of dispute resolution be termed 'healthy' and 'essential'? What kinds of 'social disputes' do khaps seek to 'resolve', after all? If there is a 'dispute' over Dalits' occupancy of land, for instance, can a Jat-dominated khap have any right to 'resolve' such a dispute? Yadav says khaps should not resolve disputes by 'listening to only one community'. But does that mean that Jat-dominated khaps can resolve disputes as long as they 'listen' to Dalits?

Khap panchayats in Haryana command enough political clout to get laws passed by the assemblies in Punjab and Haryana against women's right to inherit property (the laws were eventually denied presidential assent). What if there is a dispute between brothers and sisters over inheritance—can such openly patriarchal khaps be allowed to 'resolve' such a dispute?

Can it really be acceptable for a khap to summon an intercaste or sagotra couple to its panchayat, to 'hear' its 'opinion' on a 'dispute' regarding their marriage? Can we really pretend that khaps do not command terror over such couples? Such couples cannot even count on the police to protect them, since the police, too, hold the khaps to be 'healthier' than the courts when it comes to 'disputes' over marriage, and consider it 'socially disruptive' for people to approach the courts to assert their rights as individuals. If khaps are allowed by the government to retain such unrestrained social power and legitimacy, is it not inevitable that the killings of couples and violence against Dalits will go on?

In Haryana, it is only the Left and the women's movement that have taken on the khap panchayats. The Janwadi Mahila Samiti (JMS), with Jagmati Sangwan as its leader, is known for its consistent struggle to support couples who defy the khaps, and bring perpetrators of honour crimes to justice. The JMS played a leading role in supporting Seema and Chanderpati in their struggle for justice for Manoj and Babli.[14]

Khaps are often portrayed as medieval institutions, a 'backward' hangover that is out of place in 'modern' society. But the fact is that the power the khaps enjoy is kept in place and reproduced by economic and political structures that are all too modern.

In the anti-rape movement in December 2012 in Delhi, women raised the slogan, '*Khap se bhi azaadi, baap/bhai se bhi azaadi*' (freedom from khaps and freedom from fathers and brothers too). That slogan is rich in insight, reflecting a recognition that khaps are not just aberrant institutions found in Haryana or rural India. The women recognized 'khaps' all around them in various guises—in their own homes, their hostel administrations, their caste and community structures, their own parents and brothers—seeking to take away their freedom in the name of their safety. That slogan displayed an instinctive recognition of the fact that patriarchy doesn't rest only in rapist strangers, but in structures of caste, class and community. By choosing 'khap' as the symbol for patriarchy, the slogan recognized that the same structures that oppress women oppress Dalits too. Men and women alike raised that slogan, recognizing that patriarchy, like khaps, seeks to discipline and control women's sexuality by laying down moral diktats for women, and profiling, demonizing and even killing men of 'other' or 'forbidden' castes and communities. They recognized the 'khap' in the IPC Section 377 that profiled and criminalized gay and transgender people. The women recognized the khaps lurking in their discriminatory hostel curfews; and in their parents' anxiety to get them married into the 'right' caste; in the daily, obsessive policing by their own loved ones, of their friendships, their movements, their sexuality, all in the name of their 'safety'. So, they located the oppressiveness of 'khaps' in the normal and everyday patriarchal restrictions and codes—not simply in the shock of spectacular 'honour killings'.

When political parties support and perpetuate the power of the khaps, they are not only supporting the crimes committed by these specific institutions, but are also helping keep in place the entire web of patriarchal and caste power that strangulates the autonomy and dignity of women, Dalits and LGBTQ persons.

'He Should Have Realized His Birth-based Limitations'

In recent years, organized political violence against inter-caste marriages involving Dalit men has intensified in Tamil Nadu.

Of course, the opposition to such marriages is nothing new in India, nor is violence against Dalit communities to avenge such marriages. In fact, violence against Dalit men and their communities on the pretext of avenging both 'cow slaughter' and 'inter-caste marriage' is what has provided the template for similar violence against Muslims and interfaith marriages involving Muslim men.

The SARI (Social Attitudes Research for India) found in 2016 that 50 per cent of the non-Scheduled Caste respondents in Delhi and 70 per cent in Uttar Pradesh (UP) said that they would oppose a child or a close relative marrying a Dalit. It said:

> The survey asked respondents whether they thought there should be laws to stop marriages between upper castes and lower castes. About 40 per cent respondents in Delhi and more than 60 per cent in rural Uttar Pradesh said that such laws should exist! . . . In Delhi, about 25 per cent of highly educated people said there should be a law against such marriages; in Uttar Pradesh, it is about 45 per cent.[15]

The essay ended with the question, 'The government should be doing much more to promote inter-group marriages and to protect those who seek them . . . Will any political party have the courage to take up support for inter-caste marriages as an agenda item?'

Unsurprisingly, most parties, barring the Left, lack this courage. And then there are parties that openly and aggressively mobilize against inter-caste marriages involving Dalit men. The Pattali Makkal Katchi (PMK) of Tamil Nadu has, since 2012, sought to consolidate the intermediate Vanniyar caste (whose loyalties were scattered across various parties) and forge a broader 'backward' alliance, making inroads into the base of the Dravida Munnetra Kazhagam (DMK) and All India Anna Dravida Munnetra Kazhagam (AIADMK) by mobilizing men of intermediary castes against marriages of Dalit men with women of their communities.

In December 2012, PMK founder S. Ramadoss claimed that Dalit men 'wear jeans, T-shirts and fancy sunglasses to lure girls from other communities'.[16] The PMK's campaign began in October 2012 in the Dharmapuri district of Tamil Nadu when Ilavarasan, a young Dalit man, and Divya, a young woman from the Vanniyar caste, fell in love, eloped and got married.

The story of Ilavarasan and Divya helps us clearly see the difference in impact between parental disapproval of inter-caste marriages and organized political mobilization against these marriages.

In an interview, Ilavarasan said, 'We thought they [Divya's parents] would be angry initially but can be eventually reconciled. We simply did not expect these things to happen.'[17] In fact, in a kangaroo court organized by the Vanniyars, Divya refused to return to her parents' home and calmly stood by her marriage to Ilavarasan.

What happened then was that the PMK cadre got into action to taunt Divya's father. Instigated by them, he committed suicide (many have raised doubts about whether it was a suicide or a murder) and the PMK promptly used his suicide as a pretext to set three Dalit villages in Dharmapuri on fire. Divya was then separated from Ilavarasan. Eventually, she succumbed to the pressure exercised by the PMK on her mother and herself, and announced that she would not return to Ilavarasan, though she would always love him. Later, Ilavarasan's body was found near a railway track and a CB–CID inquiry declared it to be a suicide, though Sampath Kumar, head of the forensic medicine department and vice-principal of the Sri Ramachandra Medical College and Research Institute in Chennai, who examined Ilavarasan's body, said definitively that 'even if we don't have enough to prove that Ilavarasan was murdered, we have enough to show that he did not commit suicide'.[18]

Had there been no political interference, Divya might have overcome the disapproval of her parents much more easily. But instead, the rabble-rousing very likely led to Divya's father's suicide—and that tragedy was then used as fodder for a campaign that ended up unleashing violence and creating the emotional pressure and guilt that Divya was unable to withstand.

In another incident in Tamil Nadu, twenty-one-year-old Dalit youth Gokulraj was reportedly hacked to death in October 2015 for speaking to a girl from the intermediate Gounder caste in a Thiruchengode temple. The main accused in the murder is Yuvaraj, leader of the Dheeran Chinnamalai Gounder Peravai—a

Gounder organization. The Kongu Nadu Jananayaga Katchi (KJK), a party aiming to consolidate a Gounder base, also weighed in on the incident. In an interview, K. Gopal Ramesh, the Tamil Nadu convener of the KJK, said:

> As a Dalit, he [Gokulraj] should have understood his birth-based limitations. We all should maintain the 'Lakshman rekha' for a peaceful coexistence. We in the Kongu Vellalar caste take a lot of pride in our women. The girls in our families are our 'princesses'. We nourish them and pamper them since they are the ones who nourish our traditions and customs. How could you expect us to get this sullied? I consider that education for a girl beyond the age of nineteen pollutes her and her family. It gives them [girls and their parents] a false sense of financial security and a high social status. But, unfortunately, what they fail to realize is that it [education] threatens the very existence of our caste's pride and decorum. We are spreading the message of 'caste purity' and individual discipline among our youngsters . . . Girls' education should be encouraged only up to the age of eighteen. They should be married off then. Those who wish to pursue higher studies can do so after getting married . . . I am not justifying the death of Gokulraj. But at the same time, we will never permit any act that pollutes us.[19]

It would be wrong to label the PMK or the KJK as 'lunatic fringe' groups. While these are relatively small parties in

Tamil Nadu, they hold considerable influence. Both the PMK and the KJK supported the BJP and Narendra Modi in the 2014 parliamentary elections. In 2017, the KJK merged with the BJP.[20] The PMK allied with the BJP in the 2019 parliamentary elections as well. The Tamil Nadu government, too, had acted to protect neither Dalits from violent mobs nor inter-caste couples. The AIADMK government under the then chief minister J. Jayalalithaa had unleashed a crackdown on the Dalits of Dharmapuri when they wanted to observe a memorial day in July 2014 on the first anniversary of Ilavarasan's death. Dalits were arrested and charged under the National Security Act, their villages were surrounded and raided by a huge police force, and eventually only Ilavarasan's family members were allowed to pay their respects to his memory.

Shameless Women, Shy Women

In a 2014 tweet, S. Gurumurthy, a co-convener of the Rashtriya Swayamsevak Sangh (RSS) organization Swadeshi Jagaran Manch (and appointed a part-time director of the RBI by the Modi government) expressed the Sangh's version of the 'either Madonna or whore' categorization in a catchy phrase. He tweeted: 'Few shamelss [sic] women speak for shy women. Target is to make a shy society shameless [sic]. The more shameless one is the more modern he or she is.'[21] Gurumurthy, here, is branding feminists who demand and assert autonomy as 'shameless' (*besharam*), while the 'shy women' are, of course, the good women. In a sense, he is right. The women who raised slogans demanding fearless freedom on the streets in December 2013–14, or the ones who reject patriarchal restrictions packaged as 'safety', are, in fact, 'shame-less'. They assert their freedom from the special burden of shame, which our cultures and languages describe as a desirable attribute for women. Hindi–Urdu uses the term '*sharam–haya*' or '*naari sulabh lajja*' to describe the shyness that is supposed to define women. In Tamil, *naanam* (coyness/shyness) is described as one of the four essential virtues of women, along with *acham* (timidity), *madam* (innocence) and *payirpu* (aversion to men other than one's husband), as the adornments of a woman. The women who assert the right to loiter on the streets and protest discriminatory hostel rules[22] are, in fact, declaring that there is no shame in women seeking pleasure, risk, adventure and freedom; that rape is not a punishment for 'shamelessness'; and that, in fact, shame should be allocated to those who are violent to women and deny them equality.

Shamelessness is a quality women should embrace with pride. I was lucky to have a dad who poked fun at the notions of women needing to display '*acham naanam payirpu madamai*' and walk with eyes modestly downcast, and, instead, brought up his daughters quoting the Tamil poet Subramania Bharati, who celebrated modern women who 'walked with her head held high/Looking everyone boldly in the eye'.[23] Bharati had declared that rather than 'shyness and fear', it was '*veera sutantiram*' (brave freedom) that better suited women![24] Bharati died in 1921—but unlike many of his contemporaries, he made a conscious choice to stand by women who wanted 'brave freedom'. Today, nearly a century after Bharati's passing, here we are, still struggling to make our country and society realize that 'brave freedom'—fearless freedom—is our birthright as women and human beings.

If women are 'naturally' shy and modest, why the need to keep reminding them that they must be shy and modest? If 'lajja' (shame) is really 'naari sulabh' (that which comes easily to women), why do women keep needing to be 'disciplined' for their lack of shame? If 'shyness' and 'modesty' are descriptions of women's nature, why is it that so much energy is expended by the gatekeepers of patriarchy on prescribing shyness and modesty to women?

Today, the RSS and its outfits use violence to try and discipline women whom they see as autonomous—i.e., in their eyes, wayward and shameless.

Organized Political Terror against Interfaith Couples

Any random Internet search with the keywords 'Bajrang Dal', 'ABVP' and 'Valentine's Day' will come up with news items, year after year, where these outfits ritually harass and humiliate lovers on Valentine's Day, often getting them to forcibly tie the rakhi to declare the couple brother and sister.

In 2006, Vishwa Hindu Parishad (VHP) strongman Babu Bajrangi of Gujarat boasted to a journalist of having 'rescued' 918 women from his Hindu Kadwa Patel caste who had eloped to marry men outside their caste or faith. He used the stark image of daughters as bombs to make his point:

In every house there is a live bomb that can erupt at any time. Do you know who that is? Daughters are the honour of the family and the community, and to protect that is our Hindu duty and Hindu culture. . . . Come, and let's unite to save bombs . . . I don't believe in love marriage. We have to marry within our own community. These girls go to college, make friends with some *lafanga* [loafer], roam with them on their bikes, fall in love, and then run off and get married . . . We bring them back and convince them that they are ruining their future. They stay with me for a while and then return to their parents.[25]

This was the same Babu Bajrangi who was caught on the Tehelka sting operation boasting that he 'felt like Maharana Pratap' after committing gruesome murders of Muslims, including that of a pregnant Muslim woman in the 2002 Gujarat pogrom.[26] Bajrangi, who terrorized and inflicted violence upon Hindu women to keep them captive as properties of their castes and communities, was unsurprisingly eager to inflict violence on women as well as men of the 'enemy' community. Bajrangi was convicted and sentenced to life imprisonment in 2012[27] and released on bail in 2019.[28]

In 2006, the term 'love jihad' was not yet in vogue. But Bajrangi's imagery of the beti as bomb was trying to do exactly what the term 'love jihad' does: try to link patriarchal surveillance and violence against daughters with a spurious anti-Muslim brand of 'nationalism'. For Bajrangi and the Sangh Parivar, the borders of castes and faiths need to be policed for infiltration from the enemy with as much vigilant surveillance as the borders of the nation. Just as the Sangh drew invisible 'borders' in cities like Ahmedabad, marking Muslim ghettoes as 'Pakistans', Bajrangi is trying to mark the borders of every (Hindu) family as the border of (an imaginary Hindu) nation in microcosm. He wants Hindus to feel, however, that the borders of their family and community are lined with explosives from within. In Bajrangi's imagery, the focus is not on the Muslim 'jihadi' seducer alone, it is on the daughter herself, whose sexuality is the source of terror, who is the bomb that might explode at any time. And the unruly sexuality of daughters, every time it breaches the borders of caste and faith, calls into question the very foundation of racial purity on which the 'cultural nationalism' of the 'Hindu *rashtra*' (Hindu nation) rests.

Bajrangi's Gujarat model of terror against women has by now been replicated all over India.

In October 2015, the media portal Cobrapost released recordings of its sting operation.[29] This sting operation caught (on secret camera) a range of leaders from the BJP and a variety of Hindu majoritarian outfits explaining in detail how their network works all over the country to separate Hindu women from their Muslim lovers/husbands.

For example, in that sting operation, one leader, Sanjay Agarwal, who had been a BJP candidate in municipal elections in Muzaffarnagar, explained how they got Hindu women to disown their relationships with Muslim men: 'If she doesn't listen to us, we hit her. We get her beaten up.

We misbehave (*poori badtameezi karte hain*). Such a girl is treated with a wooden board (*bilkul, phatte se bajwate hain*). Are we wrong to do so?' Another leader, BJP MLA Suresh Rana, explained how violence is used to force a Hindu woman to agree to falsely accuse her Muslim boyfriend or husband of rape:

> A girl is a girl after all. It has always been said about them that they change in five minutes according to the circumstances ... They insist, 'No matter what, I will stay with him. I won't go without him.' If she is taken aside and given two slaps, then she herself goes and gets the FIR registered claiming, 'They sexually assaulted me ... He has been doing it for a month.' Then she will tell the whole story and slap a case on him. You can mould a girl the way you want.[30]

Ravish Tantri, the chief of Hindu Unity Forum in Kerala, made open threats to kill interfaith couples:

> When the girl goes from the 'conversion centre' to the court, we warn her that if she does not give a statement on her parents side and does not marry the guy prescribed by us, then the moment she and her husband step out of the court, they will be killed by our people.[31]

BJP MLA Sangeet Som describes how his followers exert emotional pressure on Hindu women to make them renounce Muslim husbands: 'Most importantly, we exert on her emotionally that her mother will die, her father will die and brother might even commit suicide as he would not be able to face the society.'

Agarwal states that lawyers who are also RSS members act as their informants:

> A lot of advocates are *swayam sevaks* ['volunteers' or members of the RSS]. They keep an eye to see if a Hindu girl registers at the city magistrate or the SDM's office for marriage and the date given. They find out who her lawyer is and if she is in the lawyer's chamber. Then they call us. We go there with our whole team . . . fifty, sixty, seventy people.[32]

The Cobrapost sting also revealed how, in Kerala, the Hindu Helpline offers services of administering drugs to girls who have been 'rescued' from 'love jihad'. These drugs cause temporary amnesia and are used to bring the girl under control if she is 'being too aggressive', said Cijiith from the Hindu Helpline in Ernakulam, Kerala. He claimed that parents brought their daughters from as far away as UP and Maharashtra for 'treatment' in Ernakulam, where the women were held captive and drugged in a hospital.

Jagdish Shenava, a lawyer and the VHP's Mangalore district working president, said interfaith marriages may be legal but his organization is still committed to preventing them: 'Legally, it is right, but in that there is no legality for us. We won't allow.' The BJP member of the state legislative council (MLC) in Mangalore, Captain Ganesh Karnik, said that even the police in a Congress-ruled state backed them because it was infiltrated with RSS workers: 'We have tried to send some of our boys into police. So, when we need help there are a lot of *karyakarta*s, RSS [sic]. Sixty per cent of the young constables are our students.'

Few, perhaps, can withstand such organized political violence. In the few cases where women's parents support them, of course, the political terror is foiled.

When I was in my twenties, I recall a couple of my friends planning to get married. The woman was Hindu, the man Muslim, and both went to the registrar's office to apply to get married the next month. The same night, the woman's father got a call from a stranger, asking him if he knew his daughter was eloping with a Muslim man. The father, to his great credit, was furious with the caller, and insisted on pursuing the marriage application in the registrar's office himself, and pointedly distributed sweets in the office on the wedding day. But the point is— someone in that office was trying to instigate opposition to interfaith marriages. If the father had happened to respond by opposing the marriage, surely the Sangh outfits would have descended on him to try and separate the couple and whip up communal tension.

Such violence has only got bolder in recent years. In December 2017, Mansoor Harhat Khan, an MBA, married Nupur Singhal, a doctor, at a Ghaziabad court under the Special Marriage Act and held a reception at Nupur's parents' house in Ghaziabad. The BJP Ghaziabad city president, Ajay Sharma, led a mob waving BJP and Bajrang Dal flags and shouting menacing slogans to protest outside the house. Sharma declared that the families had not taken 'permission' to hold the marriage and it was a case of 'love jihad'! Pushpendra Kumar, the father of the bride, told the press that he had been 'receiving phone calls for the last two days to stop this marriage' but had decided to stand by his daughter's decision and organize the reception.[33]

The same forces also unleash pressure on Hindu victims of 'honour killings', trying to brand Muslims rather than patriarchy as the problem. When Ankit Saxena of Delhi was killed by the family members of his Muslim girlfriend, various Sangh outfits tried to use the incident to sow anti-Muslim hatred and harvest violence. Ankit's friends and his father, Yashpal Saxena, stood tall and dignified in grief—determined to fight hatred rather than fuel it. Four months after Ankit's murder, Saxena organized an iftar with his Muslim, Sikh and Hindu neighbours, inviting them to join Muslims in breaking the Ramzan fast.[34]

But for women whose parents are not so supportive, the political terror, custodial torture and violence unleashed upon them, on top of parental and community opposition, can be overwhelming. The community and communal groups that oppose inter-caste and interfaith love treat women as the 'property' of the caste or the community, rather than as individuals with the right to take decisions for themselves. What does it take to stand up to such violence?

3
Profiles in Courage

In the face of such immense family and community pressure, compounded by a hostile and violent political climate, it takes extraordinary courage for women to stand their ground.

Alok Dhanwa's poem *Bhagi Hui Ladkiyan* has a powerful line: 'How visible the shackles of the home become/When a girl runs away from home' (घर की जंजीरें/कितना ज्यादा दिखाई पड़ती हैं/जब घर से कोई लड़की भागती है). The shackles, always present but disguised and invisible, become visible only when a daughter exercises her autonomy and falls in love. But when political forces in India today reinforce those shackles, running away is not easy.

Shalu: The Mayella of Meerut

In the first week of August 2014, the 'Meerut love-jihad case' exploded in print, electronic and social media. In video interviews to the media, twenty-year-old Shalu, an English teacher at a madarsa in the Sarawa village of Meerut, UP, said she had been held captive in madarsas, gang-raped and forced to convert to Islam. Based on her statement, several Muslim men were arrested. Several news media reported that Shalu's fallopian tubes were missing and had been removed in an operation. The truth emerged later that she had been operated upon for an ectopic pregnancy.

The Sangh and the BJP in August 2014 were still heady from the dramatic victory of Narendra Modi in the May that year. For their cadres, the Meerut 'love-jihad' case was just the fodder they needed to whip up a frenzy of prejudice and violence directed at the Muslim minority. Large crowds of cadres of various Sangh outfits, including the BJP, the VHP, the Bajrang Dal and the Hindu Behen Beti Bachao Sangharsh Samiti, held menacing rallies, raising slogans that intimidated and threatened Muslims. The ABVP formed the Meerut Bachao Manch to 'raise awareness' among Hindu girls about 'love jihad'. The case ticked all the hate-campaign boxes: a young Hindu woman 'victim', Muslim male 'rapists', madarsas as dens of 'forced conversion' and violation of Hindu womanhood, and rallying cries to save Hindu daughters from Muslim 'love-jihadi' predators. The young Muslim man, in these campaigns, was cast simultaneously as a lustful seducer and a dangerous jihadi. The Hindu woman, of course, was always cast as a gullible victim, incapable of knowing her mind, needing obsessive surveillance and control to keep her safe from Muslim seducer–terrorists.

On 30 August, less than a month after the Meerut 'love-jihad' case sensation broke in the media, journalist Neha Dixit (on behalf of Al Jazeera) visited Shalu's home and spoke to her. Dixit found that Shalu, far from being a gullible girl, was a confident young woman, who 'had financially supported her family since the age of fifteen by taking tuitions in the neighbourhood'.[1] However, Dixit found that Shalu was being held captive in her home; her mobile phone had been confiscated to prevent her from communicating with anyone without her parents' permission and surveillance. Shalu told Dixit that she had met Kaleem through a friend and fallen in love with him, especially because he was so supportive of her ambitions as a teacher.

She said that when she discovered she had an ectopic pregnancy, Kaleem and she registered themselves in a government hospital as husband and wife, and Kaleem paid for the surgery. But when her mother discovered the surgery, the whole story came out. Shalu decided she wanted to marry Kaleem, and that the most hassle-free way of doing so was for her to convert to Islam so that she and Kaleem could get married the Muslim way. The Special Marriage Act that allows for interfaith marriages is difficult for such couples because it requires a month's public notice, allowing irate parents time to interfere. So Shalu converted to Islam and adopted the name of Bushra just to get married. She told Dixit that Kaleem had assured her she could continue to keep her Hindu faith. But her parents found out and took the help of Sangh outfits to prevent the marriage. Shalu told Dixit that if she had not given a statement claiming to be a victim of rape and forced conversion, 'these people here would have killed me'. Her August statement, then, was a custodial confession obtained by custodial coercion and torture. Shalu said she loved Kaleem and wanted to marry him and passionately blamed her parents for involving politicians and the media.

Shalu also expressed the fear that she might be killed, as are so many in so-called honour crimes in the country. Al Jazeera and Dixit stayed the publication of the interview, however, fearing that it might endanger Shalu, who was still in the custody of her family. The story was only published, along with an audio recording of the conversation in October 2014, after Shalu escaped from her parents' home to the local police station and declared that she was in love with Kaleem. Shalu told the police that she had made her August statement out of fear and coercion, that her life was in danger from her family, and that her father had taken money from a BJP leader to turn a love affair into a 'love-jihad' case.

Take a moment now to imagine the kind of courage it cost Shalu to come forward and tell her truth. To confess to interfaith love, premarital sex, pregnancy and abortion would have been hard enough as it is in western UP. To do so when in the full glare of media publicity, defying not only her parents but the political forces that rule the country, is nothing short of heroic.

In *To Kill A Mockingbird*,[2] the iconic novel about an innocent black man falsely accused of raping a white woman, the defence lawyer Atticus Finch gently and compassionately invites the white woman Mayella to 'tell us what happened'—to confess that, starved of companionship and friendship, she had, in fact, embraced the accused black man, and had been beaten up by her father when he caught her, and had only claimed 'rape' under pressure from him. But Mayella was unable to tell the truth—a sexual encounter between a white woman and a black man, even if it were a public secret that all recognized, could not be acknowledged openly. But Shalu, the Mayella of Meerut, did speak the truth. She ran away from a home that had become her prison.

Shalu and Kaleem married in 2015. But the media channels that had painted Kaleem as a rapist and spread the 'love-jihad' myth, avoided setting the record straight. In December 2015, Sourodipto Sanyal wrote in Newslaundry that the worst offender, Zee News, that had spread lurid, sensational stories about 'love jihad' without a shred of evidence, never admitted it was wrong about the Meerut case.[3] Most other media too (with just a couple of exceptions) failed to hold the BJP and the RSS leaders accountable for having cynically endangered Shalu's life and the freedom of Kaleem and members of his family and community just to create grist for their hateful 'love-jihad' mill.

Hadiya's *Swathanthryam*

To me, twenty-four-year-old Hadiya's story is most remarkable for how she showed our society a mirror, in which she emerged with a dignity, grace and honesty that various hallowed institutions failed to display and uphold. Our courts and judges come out of this story looking like petty, insecure patriarchs, while Hadiya stands tall and inspires.

Hadiya converted from the Hindu faith to Islam and changed her name from Akhila to Hadiya. Her father—like so many parents in India—refused to accept that this was her own decision, and repeatedly petitioned the Kerala High Court, alleging that his daughter was a victim of a forced conversion racket. The Kerala High Court threw out his petitions twice—on the obvious grounds that Hadiya was an adult capable of taking decisions on her own. His third petition, however, was entertained by the Kerala High Court, which began scrutinizing Hadiya's life and her decisions.

Meanwhile, Hadiya placed an advertisement on a matrimonial website and chose to marry Shafin Jehan. The Kerala High Court, in an appalling verdict, annulled the marriage. It rejected Hadiya's plea that she was an adult, declaring that 'as per Indian tradition, the custody of an unmarried daughter is with the parents, until she is properly married. We consider it the duty of this court to ensure that a person under such a vulnerable state is not exposed to further danger . . . A girl aged 24 years is weak and vulnerable, capable of being exploited in many ways'. Note: this is a legal document, not a colloquial drawing-room conversation. The use of the word 'girl' rather than 'woman' is therefore a deliberate one, intended to infantilize adult Indian women. The use of the word 'properly' is also quite telling. Hadiya's marriage to Shafin is 'improper' because her father did not, in the words of his counsel, 'give away his daughter in marriage and ensure that the person who marries her is a suitable person'.

The Kerala High Court verdict also displayed an Islamophobic bias against conversion, declaring that '[It] is not normal for a young girl in her early 20s, pursuing a professional course, to abandon her studies and to set out in pursuit of learning an alien faith and religion'. Ask yourself, what if the young woman had abandoned her studies in order to marry a man of her father's choice: would the court have considered it normal or abnormal? What if she had joined a Hindu ashram: would the court have found it abnormal? Or did the court's perception of Islam as 'alien' influence its decision? As in the so-called Meerut 'love-jihad' case, various channels were emboldened by the Kerala High Court verdict to run 'audio tapes' claiming to expose 'love jihad'.[4]

Jehan appealed in the Supreme Court against the Kerala High Court verdict. But the Supreme Court, which had, not long ago, given a landmark verdict on the Right to Privacy as a constitutional right, faltered for long months when called upon to uphold Hadiya's right to privacy and autonomy. It seems that the wisest lose their heads when they taste the potent potion of Islamophobia and patriarchal paternalism.

Advocates representing Jehan and Hadiya asked the Supreme Court to stay the Kerala High Court order, ensure Hadiya's immediate freedom from parental custody and hear Hadiya's own version of events to determine whether

her conversion and marriage were a result of force. Instead, the Supreme Court allowed the order annulling Hadiya's marriage and ordering her into parental custody to stand, and, to top it all, ordered the National Investigative Agency (NIA) to investigate for evidence of a forced conversion racket!

The then chief justice, J.S. Khehar, referred to Hadiya as a 'child', and when asked not to do so, smilingly said 'for us she is a child'.[5] Again, such language in a courtroom is not casual or accidental—it is part of an insidious agenda of infantilization of adult women. The use of this word by the chief justice was as though the Supreme Court of India had, like a neighbourhood 'uncle', patted young Indian women on the head, called them 'beti' and told them they mustn't bother their little heads with serious decisions that are better left to their dads.

Hadiya remained in her father's custody for seven months, from May to November 2017. The Supreme Court, which could have freed Hadiya in August, did not even agree to summon her till November, in spite of the fact that Hadiya was clearly a prisoner in her own home, prevented from meeting her friends. She had even told the only visitor permitted, right-wing ideologue Rahul Easwar, that her life was in danger from her father's violence.

When the Supreme Court finally summoned Hadiya in November 2017, it was still reluctant to let her speak. Instead, the judges rambled on about 'Stockholm syndrome', asking, 'If we proceed with interviewing the girl in question, would that not amount to the court accepting that there has been no indoctrination and that she had consented to converting to Islam for the marriage with her free consent, in a competent state of mind?'[6] They talked about her in her presence, as if indeed she were a child incapable of understanding adult matters. Hadiya's lawyer, Indira Jaising, urging the judges to hear Hadiya as she was an adult woman with agency and who wanted to speak to them, asked if she would have been treated the same way if she had been a man. The judges responded with derision, with the then chief justice Dipak Misra asking, 'Where does gender come into this?'[7] Indeed, the judges' inability to see that no court would ever declare that the custody of an unmarried son lay with his parents was a huge part of the problem. The judges denied seeing the enormous elephant in the room—gender.

When the judges finally agreed to question Hadiya, and asked her what her dreams for the future were, she answered, 'I want freedom [she used the Malayalam word "swathanthryam"].'[8] Her words echo the Subramania Bharati poem I quoted in the second chapter, which valued and cherished veera sutantiram—brave freedom in women.[9]

For Hadiya to have stood firm after months of mental torture in her father's custody was truly inspiring. She told the media later that her father had got representatives of a 'yoga centre' (which is actually an anti-conversion clinic to coerce women who converted from Hinduism to Christianity or Islam, or married men from these faiths, to return to their faith and renounce their partners) to try and coerce her to renounce Islam and Jehan. This is a 'yoga centre' where many other women have complained of being confined and tortured to renounce their Christian or Muslim husbands.[10] It is also the place where Athira, too, had spent time, after which she converted back to Hinduism from Islam—it was Athira's allegations of forced conversion that television channels had aired as 'love-jihad tapes'.[11] In spite of the many testimonies against this 'yoga centre', courts that have been so willing to order NIA probes into 'love-jihad' bogeys in spite of women's vehement denials, have yet to order a probe of this institution.

An exchange between Hadiya and the Supreme Court judges is especially telling. The court asked her to live in a hostel and complete her studies, and asked, 'Who do you want as your guardian?' To this, she replied, 'My husband. I want someone who accepts me as Hadiya.' On hearing this, Justice Chandrachud decided to lecture Hadiya on feminist principles, saying, 'No husband is a wife's guardian. I am not my wife's guardian.' Justice Chandrachud did not see fit to tell his own brother judges of the Supreme Court and the Kerala High Court that they had no business recommending or appointing 'guardians' for adult women!

Eventually, on 8 March 2018—the hearing coincided with International Women's Day—the Supreme Court did set aside the Kerala High Court order, stating that the Kerala High Court was wrong to annul Hadiya's marriage and that she was 'at liberty to pursue her future endeavours'. Justice Chandrachud said, 'If she [Hadiya] has no issues [with the marriage], that's the end of the issue.'[12] But Hadiya made it clear repeatedly to the Kerala High Court, on record, that she had married Jehan of her own choice. Why did the Supreme Court delay for months before hearing Hadiya? Why, even after hearing Hadiya, did it delay for several more months—from November 2017 to

March 2018—before setting aside the Kerala High Court order and upholding Hadiya's choice to marry Jehan?

Was the deliberately long delay, first in hearing Hadiya and freeing her from parental custody and then in upholding her marriage, perhaps intended to wear her down in the hope that she might change her mind? We have seen how, in so many honour-crime cases, women forcibly confined in parental custody lose the will to fight and, exhausted, recant their earlier statements and say what their custodians demand they say. Hadiya survived months of confinement, isolation and torture, and retained her clear vision that what she wanted was her 'swathanthryam'. It is ironic that our country's courts are willing to entertain fantastic conspiracy theories about the brainwashing or the seducing of Hindu women by Islamic terrorist recruiters—without any evidence to back them—but the same courts are unable to recognize that a woman held in forced parental custody is vulnerable to brainwashing and torture! Hadiya's courage and clarity of vision should shame our honourable judiciary: she knew what they took so long to acknowledge—that it was her swathanthryam, her freedom, not 'national security', that was at stake.

The fact that the Supreme Court allowed a fishing expedition by the NIA into the marriage of two consenting adults and the decision of an adult woman to convert to play out for so long should worry all Indian women. The Supreme Court merely sounded regretful that it could not overrule a woman's choice—it expressed no concern or criticism that the liberty of a young adult woman was taken away and she was made a prisoner in her father's home by the order of a court.

Kausalya: Freedom Fighter against Caste

In 2015, eighteen-year-old Kausalya from Tamil Nadu married V. Shankar, whom she had met and fallen in love with at an engineering college. Shankar was a Dalit and Kausalya was from the dominant Thevar caste, and so Kausalya had to defy her furious parents to marry Shankar.

On 14 March 2016, a shocking video went viral. CCTV footage from Udumalpettai showed Kausalya and Shankar emerging from a shop together (she had just bought him a shirt for a college function) and walking towards a bus stand. As soon as they reached the main road, assailants rode up on motorbikes and attacked the couple with sickles. Shankar was killed on the spot. Kausalya, severely injured, was hospitalized.

Kausalya knew it was her parents who had ordered the killing. She knew because they had told her that they would have her and Shankar killed. She knew because they had abducted and tortured her many times since her marriage.

Kausalya's story is similar to that of so many other women. What is new are the insights she gained from her experience—into the cruelty inherent in the caste system, and the difference between love based on mutual respect and love subject to control.

Speaking to Vincent Raj, the executive director of Evidence, the organization that supported Kausalya's struggle after Shankar's murder, she said, 'My family always loved me. I was their "pet" daughter. My father got me everything I asked for. At the same time, I was barred from stepping out of the house. I wasn't allowed to speak to anyone as well. I am not sure when exactly this became the norm, but I guess that's how it had always been; perhaps since my birth.'[13]

Remember the National Family Health Survey data we read in the first chapter?[14] Kausalya's story brings that data to life. Love for a daughter in India's caste-ridden society translates all too often into surveillance and confinement by parents.

As Kausalya speaks about Shankar, it is easy to see why she fell in love with him: his respect for her personhood and autonomy shines through. It was his respectful acceptance of her rejection of his offer of love that first drew Kausalya to him. She said, '[He] wasn't angry when I rejected his love. I liked that about him. We began to have friendly conversations . . . Shankar had a special habit: he always maintained a safe distance with his women friends, treating them with lot of respect and dignity.'[15]

Shankar did not behave as though he were entitled to Kausalya's love. He did not indulge in any macho displays of aggression or Devdas-like grief to manipulate her or make her feel guilty or obliged to love him. He did not act as though she owed him love. Instead, he respected her decision but told her quietly that he still liked her a lot. That won Kausalya over: 'I had reasons for not refusing him the second time. Beyond love, I had developed respect for him as well. Shankar made me realize that dignified and respectful behaviour is the way of love.'[16]

Kausalya's family got to know of her friendship with Shankar and began abusing him and preparing to get her married to someone else. Left to themselves, she and

Shankar would have got married after completing their studies and finding jobs. But now, worried that they might be forcibly separated, they decided to get married. Kausalya would work and support Shankar till he finished his own studies and got a job, they decided. So, they had a simple temple wedding with the help of Shankar's friends.

Kausalya's memories of Shankar contain small details that are very moving, and give us a clear picture of what kind of a man he was. She said, in a voice choked with emotion, 'I had never done housework, so Shankar was the one who cooked for me. Even before he was killed, he was telling me that he is going to make pooris for me that night.'[17] Elsewhere, Kausalya had this to say, 'For those eight months that I lived with him, he was more motherly than my mother towards me. He would cook for me, wash my clothes, take care of me like a child. He did things that society considers women's chores . . . For others, love means many things. For me, love gives women self-respect.'[18]

Kausalya's family swung into action to undo the marriage, doing what so many other parents of eloping daughters do. They filed a case against Shankar, alleging he had kidnapped Kausalya. Kausalya and Shankar filed a complaint at their local police station, stating they feared harm from Kausalya's parents. The couple found, as Manoj and Babli of Haryana did, that the police supported the casteist patriarchs and not the rights of the couple. With both Kausalya's and Shankar's family members gathered at the police station, the police inspector rebuked Kausalya for defying her parents, saying, 'Love lasts for sixty days and desire for thirty! You come from a family of means. You have married a poor boy. How will you live?'[19] She stood her ground. Kausalya's aunt made her strip off all her clothes and jewellery that had been provided by her parents. She said of this experience, 'In a room at the police station where I was removing the clothes given by my family, I sensed the depravity of caste and the insult I had to undergo because of it.'[20]

At a court hearing a couple of days after her marriage, Kausalya was assaulted by her family members: 'They requested the police's permission to meet me for five minutes and surrounded me and said, "Aren't you ashamed to bear the *thali* (*mangalsutra*) tied by a Pallar guy? You better come with us or we will kill you." I turned away quietly. This angered them, and my grandmothers and my aunts got hold of my hair and started raining blows on my cheeks, on my breasts, on my back. I lost my balance and fell down.'[21]

After the court dismissed Kausalya's father's petition, she and Shankar remained afraid of her family. They slept in a different relative's house each night, avoiding his house.

Her grandfather came over as a decoy. Pretending to be on Kausalya's side, he claimed to be unwell and asked her to come with him to the hospital. Once she sat on his scooter, he abducted her and took her to her parents. They took her to four godmen and a godwoman, all of whom performed rituals to free her from a 'spell' they claimed had been cast on her. One godman prescribed potions, which her parents forced her to consume. Her aunt and parents called her a whore, beat her and burnt her thali, *metti* (toe ring) and clothes.

The police, meanwhile, cooperated with Kausalya's father. She overheard a call by a policeman to her father on the speakerphone. The cop said:

> The boy who eloped and married your daughter, and his father have lodged a complaint. Things are getting serious. Please bring your daughter. But don't worry; things will only happen according to your wishes. Come with Rs 20,000 for the inspector. Also, pressurize your daughter to say that she doesn't want to go with the boy and that she wants to return to her parents' place.[22]

Is it any surprise if many women lose their spirit and will when subjected to such abduction, imprisonment and torture at the hands of her own parents, and when betrayed by the police? What should shock us—as Hadiya's story also showed us—is that our policing and judicial mechanisms tacitly allow and participate in such torture. If such torture succeeds in producing obedience to parental and caste authority, if women relinquish their lovers or husbands as a result, our institutions seem to breathe a sigh of relief.

But Kausalya did not give up. When she kept insisting on her wish to return to Shankar, her family members said they would give her poison and kill her. She was taken to the police station. At the request of an advocate, she did not accuse her parents of kidnapping, she simply said she wanted to return with Shankar, who was at the police station waiting for her.

Next, her grandmother played the same game—pretended to be on their side, won their confidence, but then led them into a trap for her parents to abduct her again. This time, bystanders on the street helped them escape.

Next, her parents tried bribery. They came to Shankar's and Kausalya's home, and offered Shankar Rs 10 lakh to let Kausalya come home with them. Shankar, of course, refused the money, and Kausalya, too, snubbed her father, saying nothing would induce her to leave Shankar. Her father left, warning Kausalya that she and Shankar would be killed.

The day Shankar was killed, she recalls the assailants saying, 'How dare you love, you Pallar son-of-a-bitch!'[23] Kausalya, recovering from her injuries and the trauma of seeing Shankar hacked to death, struggled with grief and anger. She attempted suicide. But supported by Left, feminist and Dalit activists, she began to make sense of her world anew. She read Periyar and Ambedkar. Haunted by the fact that her parents used her grandparents to try and trap her, that they hired mercenaries to kill their daughter and son-in-law, she arrived at a profound realization: 'I thought what my parents had for me was love. I realize today that it was love for the caste.'[24] This is why Kausalya now refers to her parents by their names, Chinnasamy and Annalakshmi, refusing to acknowledge them as her father and mother.

Kausalya pursued justice for Shankar in court. Her father, Chinnasamy, and five others were sentenced to death, one to a life term and another to five years' imprisonment. Her pain and her struggle transformed her. She knows her life is still in danger. But she refuses to live in fear, and rides her Royal Enfield motorbike boldly, her hair cropped short. She sees herself as a freedom fighter against caste, saying, 'Our country got independence but we don't even have the freedom to love.'[25] She has dedicated her life to annihilating caste. She works with Dalit children, educating them, and teaching herself and them to play the *parai* drum, associated with the Dalits. She also fell in love with and married Sakthi, a fellow parai drummer and anti-caste activist, in a self-respect marriage of the kind popularized by Periyar. They wrote their own marriage vows—in which they vowed to support each other's work, to work to annihilate caste and liberate women, and to make sure the doors of their home would always be open to young couples facing societal opposition.

On Ambedkar Jayanti (14 April) in 2017, Kausalya met Divya, who had lost her husband Ilavarasan and her father to the scourge of caste. Kausalya's account of this meeting, in a Facebook post, is deeply moving. Kausalya wrote:

My respect for her [Divya] grew after the meeting. She does go to college and come back, but otherwise she still cannot step out of her home. Even if Divya sports a simple bindi and steps out, there are people who taunt her for forgetting the past. I couldn't converse with her for long, her mother was around. But when I could, I asked how she was coping with it. 'How can I so easily forget someone with whom I was so deeply in love?' Divya asked me. Confined within her house, she has no space to fight . . . Divya's mother kept insisting that her daughter was happy—that they did not want people to come only because they kept talking about the past. We actually did not want to speak about the past. All I wanted was to meet her and speak to her. I really want to keep meeting her as often as possible so I hardly spoke about the past. Only when we were leaving, I told her my own story. Divya was not aware of it.[26]

What needs to be underlined here is the utter failure of Central and state governments to support women like Kausalya. In September 2017, the office of the inspector general of registration, Tamil Nadu, issued an 'internal circular' requiring parental consent for the registration of marriages under the Hindu Marriage Act![27] This means that inter-caste couples getting married and then wanting to register their marriages will not be able to do so if the wife's parents refused consent. Such a circular shows that the government of Tamil Nadu—a state where ruling parties pay lip service to Periyar while enforcing ideas he fought all his life—is complicit in honour crimes and anti-Dalit violence.

Daughters Will Fight!

In the 'Beti Bachao' narrative, the daughter is passive, and it is for benign patriarchs—her parents, the government— to rescue her. The active verb 'bachao' (rescue) is not for the daughter: it can be appropriated by the government and by the violent caste and communal outfits alike.

When I think of daughters like Shalu, Hadiya and Kausalya, I think the slogan we need to nurture is

'*Ladegi Beti*'—daughters will fight! We need to support
and nurture the active courage of our daughters.

Neelam Katara, whose son Nitish was killed by
brothers of his girlfriend Bharti Yadav, spoke once of her
disappointment in Bharti's 'weakness'. After the murder,
Bharti had immediately reached out to Nitish's brother
to tell him that she feared her brothers had killed Nitish,
but later recanted. In court, she denied being in love with
Nitish—though she did betray emotion when faced with
the letters and cards she admitted sending him. Neelam
was saddened by Bharti's conduct:

> She couldn't deny the relationship at that point of time
> but she said that whatever was there between Nitish
> and her was just friendship. The brothers didn't know
> about it. She also said that her brothers were very loving
> and caring people who could never have done anything
> like that.[28]

I believe that every woman has both a Divya and a
Kausalya, a Bharti and a Hadiya inside her. What can we,
as a society, do to strengthen the courage and autonomy of
our daughters and sisters? What can we do to encourage
parents to feel pride rather than shame in such courageous
daughters? Divya's and Kausalya's parents were taunted by
casteists for having 'lost' runaway daughters to Dalit men—
to acknowledge this is not to absolve parents of honour
crimes, but to ask what we can do to create a supportive
community for parents whose daughters defy caste and
patriarchy. What can we do to resist the political forces

who bake their political rotis by fanning up the fire of caste patriarchy?

We need to do more than respond *after* an 'honour killing'—wherever we live, we need to create networks to support inter-caste, interfaith and same-sex relationships. We need to hold our governments accountable to defending the freedom of women and the safety of couples in such relationships. We need the quiet people—even if this is a quiet minority—who are anti-caste and anti-patriarchy to stand up, shout out to each other and be counted.

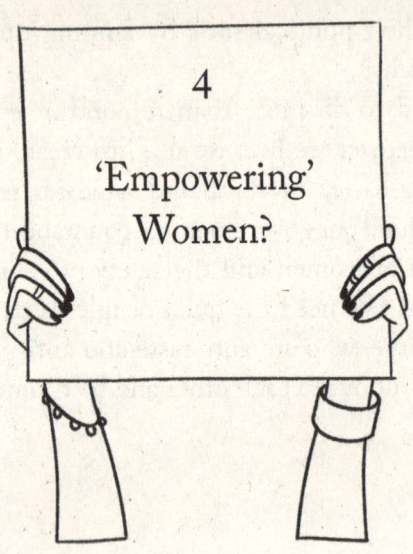

4

'Empowering' Women?

Most of us imagine that the Government of India is spending taxpayers' money and designing policies that are intended to empower women. We assume that this empowerment has not happened yet because Indian society and culture is just too set in its ways. So, 'society' and 'culture' get the blame, while our rulers say, 'Hey, we're trying, you should support us in our efforts!' The same goes for campaigns run by various international funding agencies.

In this chapter, I invite you to take a closer look at the feel-good slogans of campaigns by governments and contrast them with the slogans and goals of feminist campaigns and movements.

Beti Bachao: with Conditions Attached

In January 2015, Prime Minister Narendra Modi launched the Beti Bachao Beti Padhao (Save and Educate Daughters) scheme. The main goal of this scheme was to counter sex-selective abortions and improve the child sex ratio.

On 3 April 2018, replying to a question in the Rajya Sabha, the then minister of state for health and family welfare Anupriya Patel presented data showing that the sex ratio at birth, which was 906 in 2012–14, had dropped to 900 in 2013–15 and further to 898 in 2014–16.

There are, of course, many reasons for why a campaign might be ineffective: not least being the lack of political will of the governments to enforce the Pre-Conception and Pre-Natal Diagnostic Techniques (PCPNDT) Act 1994. The then women and child development minister Maneka Gandhi had courted controversy by suggesting that child sex determination during pregnancy be made compulsory, so that it is not doctors but the pregnant women who are surveilled and held responsible for the safety of female foetuses.[1] This, of course, is a travesty of women's rights over their own bodies and choices. Indian law recognizes that women have a right to abortion, which is why sex *determination* of the foetus by doctors is criminalized, to make sure that abortions are not sex-selective. The abysmal sex ratio in India is testimony to the fact that criminal doctors have continued with the business of prenatal sex determination. Maneka Gandhi's proposal is one that the medical lobby has been pushing for a long time. And if it were ever implemented, it would result in a dystopia in which pregnant women are treated as baby-producing machines that are the property of the state, subjected to state surveillance and prevented from having abortions unless approved by the state![2]

What should also concern us is that the message of the Beti Bachao campaign itself is steeped in the same patriarchy that it claims to be fighting. And patriarchy is one area where 'using fire to fight fire' does not work.

In June 2018, the Indian social media saw a photograph of a mural against sex selection on a wall in Haryana. The image showed a little girl, with her head covered, rolling out rotis, with the slogan '*Kaise khaoge unke haath ki rotiya, jab paida hone nahi doge betiyan?*' (Who will make rotis for you if you won't let daughters be born?). The Haryana government got considerable criticism online for this mural. Other similar slogans abound in the Beti Bachao campaign, such as '*Beti nahin bachaoge to bahu kahan se laoge*' (If you don't save daughters, where will you get daughters-in-law?) and '*Ma chahiye; behen chahiye; patni chahiye; to beti kyon nahin chahiye?*' (You want mothers, sisters, wives, then why don't you want daughters?). This sounds like an appeal to common sense, but perhaps it is not effective in curbing sex selection because it is an appeal to a patriarchal common sense. Should we be asked to appreciate daughters only as performers of domestic chores? Is a daughter's right to be born and cherished dependent on her role as a future mother/daughter/sister/daughter-in-law/wife to men?

In support of Beti Bachao, the prime minister famously endorsed the Selfie with Daughter campaign—launched by Sunil Jaglan, who was, in July 2015, the *sarpanch* of the Bibipur panchayat in Haryana—on his *Mann Ki Baat* radio show, urging fathers to show pride in their daughters by sharing selfies with their daughters on social media.

Selfie with Daughter began with Jaglan's involvement in the Avivahit Purush Sangathan (the Unmarried Men's Organization) in Haryana.[3] A woman must justify her birth by making herself available as a willing wife/daughter-in-law, who will cook, clean, give birth to and care for children. But men feel entitled to wives who will serve them and bear them kids.

Nothing drives home the utter arrogance of such patriarchal entitlement more starkly than the phenomenon of bride purchase. Jaglan complained that the men of Haryana, faced with a drought of daughters, are forced to buy wives from other states: 'A couple of months ago, a family had purchased a bride from Uttarakhand. She ran away. They bought another one, she too ran away.'[4] Jaglan implies that wives born and trained in the correct caste in Haryana and acquired in the traditional way rather than by cash purchase will not have the option of running away. After all, where would Haryana's 'own' women run to?

The Avivahit Purush Sangathan had demanded that politicians take steps to remedy the situation and ensure a supply of brides, raising the slogan '*Bahu dilao, vote pao*'

(Give us brides, get our votes). In response to such campaigns, BJP leader O.P. Dhankar had promised good brides from Bihar:

> Making the BJP strong also means that those youths in many villages who are roaming without brides will get one . . . I told them that Sushil Modi [senior BJP leader in Bihar] is a good friend of mine. We will ensure a compatible match and do away with the practice of bringing brides from any other place.[5]

Many defend such campaigns, arguing for pragmatism. People are going to continue to be patriarchal, they say so one has to appeal to their patriarchal interests to allow girls to be born. If individual patriarchal families want to avoid girls, perhaps they can be induced to allowing girls to be born in the collective interest of patriarchal society, or so the argument goes. The problem is that as long as women are devalued and denied personhood and equality, patriarchy is not particularly insecure. Brides are 'in short supply' in Haryana, but this shortage can be made good by importing from other states. As long as daughters in, say, Bihar, continue to be treated as commodities rather than persons, families will sell daughters to their counterparts in Haryana. Just as migrant labour goes from poorer to richer regions, purchased wives, too, tend to go from poorer to richer states.[6] From a pragmatic perspective, it could well be argued that a shortage of women in Haryana turns a daughter from liability to asset in Bihar, since she goes from being a 'burden' to an asset that can be sold. Is that really true? Are daughters accorded more respect when they become a saleable commodity rather than a burden that one can be rid of only by paying dowry?

The problem with many of the campaigns against sex selection is that they buy into the patriarchal excuse that families see daughters as a burden (because of dowry) and so wish to avoid having them. The thing is, families do not need to be reminded of the 'uses' of women as wives, mothers, daughters-in-law and so on—they already know this full well. The state and families both recognize the 'worth' and 'value' of women as providers of domestic services and care work. There is no one who would fail to pay lip service to the nurturing roles of women—why does sex selection persist nevertheless? Why does the state go soft on sex determination by the medical industry?

At its core, the question is, can we fight sex-selective abortion or any other form of gender discrimination and violence by appeasing patriarchy? By pandering to men's sense of patriarchal entitlement to wives and their domestic and sexual services? Or can change come only by boldly asserting the rights, equality and personhood of women and sexual and gender minorities, and fighting patriarchy lock, stock and barrel?

Remember, Jaglan's Haryana is where 'honour killings' are rampant. Nakul Sawhney's documentary *Izzatnagari ki Asabhya Betiyan* (Immoral Daughters in the Land of Honour) speaks to leaders of the dominant Jat khaps, who defend their right to violently or coercively regulate sexuality and marriage, saying: 'Some daughters who are immoral/uncivilized, like animals, try to corrupt the rest by demanding that they should be allowed to live their life without restrictions.' Does Beti Bachao really challenge such forces? Or are the khaps and the Beti Bachao campaign united in their paternalism that can be alternatively benign and violent, depending on the daughters' obedience or disobedience? Both the khaps and the Beti Bachao campaign assume that parents have a right to decide, based on their assessment of a daughter's moral worth and potential role as mother/wife/daughter-in-law, whether or not she has the right to exist. Such paternalism asks fathers/parents to take pride in daughters, recognizing that these are the future daughters-in-law, wives and mothers. But the very same paternalism wields the power to order the killing of disobedient daughters: those who decide to break caste or community barriers to marry, who are therefore unavailable to serve as wives for the 'avivahit purush' (unmarried men) of the caste and community of their birth.

Swachhata or Sexism?

The Swachh Bharat Abhiyan (Clean India Campaign) and its predecessor, the United Progressive Alliance's (UPA's) Nirmal Bharat Abhiyan against open defecation, rely heavily on shaming tactics accompanied by emotional appeals to protect women's 'honour', 'modesty' and 'safety'. Women and girls, we are told, are especially invested in building toilets at home, even selling mangalsutras and jewellery to do so, to protect them from the 'shame' and danger of open defecation. Swachh Bharat has even been described as India's 'biggest women's movement at the moment'.[7]

In his Independence Day speech in 2014, Prime Minister Modi said, 'Has it ever pained us that our mothers and sisters have to defecate in the open? Isn't the dignity of women our collective responsibility?' A Swachh Bharat advertisement prepared in collaboration with Astral Pipes shows women publicly shaming men of the village who are defecating in the open, saying that open defecation puts their honour and safety at risk.[8]

A wall graffiti in UP says '*Bahu betiyan door na jayen, ghar mein hi shauchalay banvayen*' (Daughters-in-law, daughters should not go far, construct a toilet in your house). A Swachh Bharat banner in Rajasthan has a daughter asking her mother, '*Ma, ghar mein ghoonghat tera saathi, phir kyon shauch khule mein jaati?*' (Mother, your veil is your companion in your home, so why do you defecate in the open?).[9] The Swachh Bharat campaign with Amitabh Bachchan as its brand ambassador has an advertisement[10] with an image of women accompanied by the messages: '*Inki izzat ke liye darwaza bandh*' (Close the door for their honour) and '*Jab ghar mein shauchalay banvayenge, tab ghar ki auraton ko door nahin jana padega, unhen takleef nahin hogi aur aapka man bhi halka hoga*' (When you make a toilet in your home, the women of your home won't have to go far, they won't face any trouble and your mind, too, will be lighter).

In one promotional video, Nirmal Bharat brand ambassador actress Vidya Balan is seen at a wedding where a mother-in-law is shown to be disapproving of the bride who raises her veil to take a sip of water. Soon after, the bride whispers to Balan that she needs to go to the toilet. When Balan asks where the toilet is, the mother-in-law replies there isn't one, everyone goes to the field. Balan then tells the bride, '*Bahu, phir to tum ghoonghat khol hi do*' (Daughter-in-law, then you might as well take off your veil), adding to the mother-in-law, 'You don't like your daughter-in-law to remove her veil even for a moment, and at the same time you want her to go in the open?'[11]

The Madhya Pradesh government in 2013 titled its campaign to end open defecation 'Maryada Abhiyan'.[12] The word '*maryada*' in Hindi signifies women's sense of dignity and/or womanly shame, and a campaign booklet issued by the state government harps on the theme of how open defecation threatens women's dignity and puts women in danger of sexual harassment.

A Swachh Bharat poster[13] in Muzaffarpur, Bihar, has an image of a man presenting a woman he has abducted to a villainous dacoit chief, saying, 'Here boss, I've brought this beautiful *lote-wali* (bearer of a mug of water) from the field for you', while the chief replies that today will be a day for rape.

There are four serious problems with the projection of such a message: first, it targets women alone instead of educating the whole community to give up open defecation; second, it claims to promote women's safety while, in fact, the campaign makes women less safe; third, it promotes patriarchal values of 'honour'; and fourth, it implicitly promotes victim-blaming for sexual violence. Let us take a closer look at these four problems.

First: open defecation is a life-threatening public-health crisis, that can't be solved by women alone giving it up. Pegging the campaign on toilets for women carries the message that toilets are *for women alone* and not for men. If men continue to defecate in the open, the life-threatening health problem, of course, remains.

Second, the Swachh Bharat campaign itself makes women vulnerable to sexual violence, and makes women, children, the elderly and the poor unsafe. It promotes tactics of public shaming by vigilante groups set up by the district administration. These vigilantes use whistling or clapping, naming and shaming, as tactics to publicly humiliate open defecators. Groups of women follow men and groups of men follow women when they are on their way to the fields. They grab the lotas and shout slogans. They take photos and videos of people defecating and threaten to make their names and their images/videos public. The problem is, such acts themselves constitute violence.

Section 354 of the Indian Penal Code defines the crime of voyeurism clearly. A man watching or capturing the image of a woman while she is engaging in a private act, and sharing or threatening to share such images publicly is voyeurism—a sexual crime against women. It's ironical that the Swachh Bharat Abhiyan tries to instil fear in women that open defecation will expose them to voyeurism and sexual violence—and then unleashes government-sponsored voyeurism and violence on them! The Maryada Abhiyan booklet asks people to imagine a young woman defecating in the open and being watched by voyeuristic men. It even carries a voyeuristic drawing to this effect. It asks 'sanitation monitoring committees' (which are basically vigilante mobs) to patrol villages, whistle at people defecating in the open, and take photographs and videos of open defecators 'with the threat and possibility that the photos might be displayed or the videos shown'. The district administration of then Rajasthan chief minister Vasundhara Raje's own constituency of Jhalawar in June 2016 asked teachers to conduct similar patrols and take photos and videos of open defecators.[14] The consequence of such patrols can be frightening.

When vigilante groups are emboldened to indulge in violence publicly, they can easily metamorphose into lynch mobs—especially in a political climate of impunity[15] for mobs that lynch Muslims. In July 2017, in Pratapgarh, Rajasthan, women of the Bagwasa *basti* were out in the open in the early morning when male government officials arrived to photograph and videograph them. Comrade Zafar Hussein, an activist of the Communist Party of India (Marxist–Leninist)—CPI(ML)—tried to stop them. He pointed out that the women, and he himself, had submitted memorandums and led delegations seeking funds from the government to build individual and community toilets, and ensure proper water and cleaning facilities for such toilets. When he received these memoranda, the elected chairman of the municipality—a BJP leader—tore up their memorandum and told them not to bother getting toilets made because the local administration was planning to evict the entire colony. There is a single community toilet with ten commodes in Bagwasa basti—which houses 3000 residents—which has no water, where the flushes do not work and, consequently, the commodes are clogged and unusable.[16]

Comrade Zafar paid with his life for his intervention. The Swachh campaigners lynched him to death. This is not the only instance of violence by the 'sanitation-monitoring' mobs.

An elderly man in Ujjain, Madhya Pradesh, in December 2016, for example, was beaten by civic body authorities and forced to clean his faeces with his hands, and a video of the whole degrading scene was shared by Ujjain Municipal Corporation (UMC) deputy commissioner Sunil Shah in a WhatsApp group.[17]

In Maharajpur village in Rajnandgaon district of Chhattisgarh in October 2016, Vipin Sahu was dragged out of his home, beaten and stabbed to death by a mob in front of the whole village because he had delayed construction of a toilet in his home and sought more time to do so.[18]

In August 2017, two children fleeing an early-morning Swachh Bharat patrol in Chenari village of Rohtas district, Bihar, jumped into a flooded river, Kudra, to escape. They were presumed drowned. But they survived, holding on to reeds for a couple of hours before being found and rescued by villagers. Little children from the poorest and most deprived communities are being subjected to such terror and danger by a government-backed patrol, in the name of curbing open defecation![19]

Such tactics prevailed in the UPA-era Nirmal Bharat campaign too. A report in the *Guardian* details the coercive tactics adopted by government officials in Karnataka to curb open defecation:

A local official proudly testified to the extremes of the coercion. He had personally locked up houses when people were out defecating, forcing them to come to his office and sign a contract to build a toilet before he would give them the keys. Another time, he had collected a woman's faeces and dumped them on her kitchen table.[20]

But the Modi government's Swachh Bharat mission differs from the UPA-era campaign in that it depends on neighbourhood vigilante groups at least as much as, if not more than, on government officials. The mission has been described approvingly as a success story for 'nudge economics', i.e. policies that 'nudge' people gently towards behavioural change.[21] The NITI Aayog (a government think tank) along with the Bill and Melinda Gates Foundation, had set up a 'nudge unit' to push campaigns such as Beti Bachao and Swachh Bharat.[22] The Gates Foundation even awarded Narendra Modi for the Swachh Bharat Abhiyan. Critics raising human rights violations have pointed out that access to a clean toilet cannot 'outweigh the violence and persecution (people) may face in the rest of their lives'.[23] Moreover, as we have seen in the instances cited above, the campaign did not gently 'nudge' people to change their practices: it deployed patriarchal, communal and class- or caste-based violence and persecution to shame and coerce people.

The third problem with the Swachh Bharat messaging is that it ties toilets to patriarchal notions of 'ghoonghat' (veil) and 'honour'. We saw in the first chapter how women's confinement in the four walls of the home is itself a form of violence and discrimination. Swachh Bharat, in the name of linking toilets to women's 'empowerment' and 'dignity', actually does exactly the opposite, suggesting that toilets in the home are needed to confine women inside homes. The Amitabh Bachchan 'Shut the Door' advertisement, for instance, seeks to tell *men* that they can feel reassured if their womenfolk do not have to 'go far' to defecate! So it is addressing an anxiety men feel about womenfolk 'going far'. Is this anxiety shared by women? At a meeting of my organization, the All India Progressive Women's Association (AIPWA), a comrade from Patna told us about her experience at a village in rural Bihar. As women got ready in the early mornings and late evenings to go out en masse to relieve themselves, she asked them if they wouldn't prefer to have toilets in their homes. They scoffed: '*Didi*, why give them (our men and in-laws) another reason to keep us captive indoors?! This is our only excuse to get some fresh air, take a walk together and speak to friends without someone overhearing us! We make the most of it, dragging out the outings as long as possible.'

The Sanitation Quality Use Access and Trends (or SQUAT) survey 2014 found that many women, in fact, cherished open defecation because it offered an opportunity to go out of the house: 'A young daughter-in-law in Haryana, whose household owns a latrine, explained that: the reason that [I and my sisters-in-law] go outside [to defecate] is that we get to wander a bit . . . you know, we live cooped up inside.'[24]

The fourth problem is that the campaign's patriarchal messaging implicitly legitimizes victim-blaming. The survey found that it was a myth that open defecation increases the danger of sexual violence, noting that:

Of 1046 women interviewed by the SQUAT survey, 4.3 per cent told us that while going to defecate, they had been the victim of someone attempting to molest them. Of the same group, 7.6 per cent reported that this had happened to them while going to the market . . . The point is that it is not a serious policy response to these facts to suggest that women should stop going to markets.[25]

In the light of these facts, take a fresh look at the poster from Muzaffarpur, Bihar, that used scaremongering about rape as an argument for toilets. With such posters, victim-blaming gets a 'Swachh' disguise, since it is women's presence in public spaces outside the home that is being blamed for rape and crime. Even if women stop defecating in the fields and start using toilets, can't they even go safely for a walk in the fresh air? If they are molested or raped, will the government blame them for going out walking?

Shilpa Phadke, one of the authors of the influential book *Why Loiter?*,[26] which is about the need for campaigns against sexual violence to assert women's right to 'loiter' in public spaces without reason, writes of the Swachh Bharat campaign:

That isn't to say that the call for toilets inside the home isn't a good thing. It will certainly make women significantly more comfortable. But the movement conveniently dovetails with ideologies that equate honour and dignity with women not being seen outside. Keeping women in the home also prevents their meeting 'unsuitable' men of different castes . . . My collaborative research based in Mumbai has focused on the value of public toilets as a means of enhancing women's access to public space. A number of recent reports mentioned that girls use toilets at school during terms but that those facilities are closed during vacations, hence their need to use the fields. School toilets hold the key to some transformation: The provision of public toilets (or community toilets, as they are often called) rather than private ones might solve the problems of health without restricting women to the home.[27]

How willing is the government to take on board feminist criticisms of the Swachh Bharat Abhiyan messaging? The Swachh Bharat Mission (Gramin) of the Ministry of Drinking Water and Sanitation issued a circular in April 2017, titled 'Guidelines on Gender Issues in Sanitation'. This circular noted that:

> Behaviour-change messaging in SBM-G often includes subjects like 'shame and dignity of women'. While these may be useful for entry-point messaging, they carry risks of lack of ownership by men and the reinforcing of gender-stereotypes (like women should not step out of the house, men as custodians of women's dignity, etc). The . . . messaging should, therefore, be gender-sensitive and targeted at both men and women, particularly focusing on men who are often the primary decision-makers in rural households where household expenditure is involved.

This circular is no doubt a step in the right direction. But what is conspicuously absent from the guidelines is any prohibition of the use of gendered shaming and bullying tactics and voyeuristic violence by early-morning patrols. The Bagwasa incident, where Comrade Zafar was killed for trying to stop patrols from taking photos and videos of women in Rajasthan, happened in July 2017, months after this circular was issued. It did nothing to deter the use of sexual violence to shame women for defecating in the open. All over rural India, the patriarchal messaging continues to abound. The Bihar poster using the bogey of rape, for instance, was seen in December 2017—long after these guidelines were issued by the Central government to all states. Perhaps this is because the circular itself suggests that the patriarchal messaging appealing to notions of feminine 'shame and honour' are 'useful for entry-point messaging' and not harmful in themselves. They are critiqued primarily for excluding men from the messages against open defecation, not for harming the freedom and autonomy of women.

The most important question is, why does the Swachh Bharat Abhiyan refuse to address the elephant in the room: caste? The SQUAT survey found that caste prejudices and taboos, not poverty, was the main factor deterring Indians from using small-pit toilets. Its researchers observe that 70 per cent of rural households in India do not have a toilet or a latrine, while 'in rural sub-Saharan Africa, where people are, on average, poorer, less educated, and less likely to have access to an improved water source than people in rural India, only about 35 per cent of people defecate in the open without a toilet or latrine. In rural Bangladesh, only 5 per cent of people defecate in the open.'[28]

Indians across social sections do not like using the small twin-pit latrines that have helped eradicate open defecation in poor countries the world over, because these latrines require periodic manual pit-emptying—a practice associated with manual scavenging, associated with Dalits and consequently considered degrading and polluting. Non-Dalits will not empty the pits, and Dalits no longer want to be employed to do such labour. If affordable twin-pit latrines are constructed, one of the pits can be allowed to decompose into compost while the other is in use—emptying decomposed waste is not manual scavenging. But the SQUAT survey found that it still carried the social stigma associated with degrading labour, and was thus shunned.

Remember, caste prejudices related to sanitation are by no means limited to rural, 'backward' Indians. People who are privileged enough to have flush toilets in their homes also share those prejudices, as displayed in the fact that most of them would not allow workers from oppressed castes who clean their toilets to eat or drink out of their utensils.[29]

The big, unspoken question with regard to community toilets and individual pit latrines alike is, who will clean the toilets? Campaigns like the Swachh Bharat Abhiyan do not address this question because the answer will require them to confront the reality of manual scavenging that Dalit sanitation workers are forced to perform.

If the Swachh Bharat campaigns ditched their obsession with patriarchal notions and coercive vigilante or lynch-mob tactics, and instead concentrated on democratic dialogue with people about caste, sanitation and health, they might have generated better results.

Population Control

In his Independence Day speech in 2019, Prime Minister Modi announced a 'population control' campaign projecting small families as 'patriotic'. Like the Beti Bachao and Swachh Bharat campaigns, this campaign, too, is ostensibly aimed at 'nudging' people to modify their social behaviour.

In his speech, Modi called for a campaign against what he called 'uncontrolled population growth'. The campaign, he said, would focus on projecting parents with small families as responsible and patriotic. He said, 'Before a child arrives in our family, we should think—have I prepared myself to fulfil the needs of the child? Or will I leave it dependent on society?'[30] This rhetoric shifts responsibility for the care (education, health, food and shelter) of children from the State and government to the parents. Deprivation is framed as parental neglect and irresponsibility. The ideology of 'population control' has always implied that it is poor families and poor nations that are expected to reproduce less. The fact is that population is not responsible for poverty. Wealth is not innocent of poverty. Poverty is produced by a system that exploits the poor to reward the rich. Poverty of nations is linked to a violent history of colonialism, where these nations were plundered and impoverished.

For long, the 'population control' policy of the Government of India, backed by international funding agencies, has resulted in extreme violence towards poor women in India. Fifteen women from poor and oppressed communities died in a 'sterilization camp' in Chhattisgarh in 2014.[31] Between 2009 and 2012, fifteen women died every month due to botched sterilization operations in similar camps.[32] The 'population control' campaign is now likely to boost violence on women's bodies, and shame poor women for bearing 'too many children'.

At a jan sunvai (public hearing) organized in Delhi by the Right to Food Campaign in 2016 on maternity entitlements, the chairperson of the National Commission for Protection of Child Rights (NCPCR) said that women must help themselves and not expect the government to solve their problems. When Neelam, a woman worker, was testifying about being denied maternity entitlements in her first two pregnancies, a representative of the National Commission for Women (NCW) interrupted to comment that she appeared to be pregnant for a third time. When Neelam said she was, the NCW representative began to scold her, saying: 'Don't you know better than to keep having babies? Don't you know there should be a gap of at least three years between babies?' The public hearing was meant to be a space for women to speak about how the government had failed to provide them the entitlements they needed to ensure their dignity as women and mothers. But both the NCPCR chairperson and the NCW representative sought to absolve the government of responsibility, while the latter chose to make it an occasion to blame and shame women.[33]

Quite apart from the tendency of 'population control' campaigns to inflict humiliation and violence on women, these campaigns are also likely to have a communal subtext. In Gujarat 2002, Modi had infamously called the relief camps for the pogrom-affected Muslims 'baby-producing factories'.[34] On 11 July 2019, just a month before his Independence Day speech as PM, his Cabinet minister Giriraj Singh addressed a rally in Delhi on World Population Day, demanding a Population Control Law.[35] At that rally, a song played from the dais, '*Jansankhya visphot se apni azaadi ko khatra hai/Hamko gaddaron ki badhti aabaadi se khatra hai*' (Our independence is in danger from population explosion/We are in danger from the rising population of traitors). Singh made a speech calling for a law to prevent the decline in the population of Hindus and curb the growth of the Muslim population. Participants in the rally branded Muslims as unpatriotic and irresponsible for bearing too many children even if they were poor and worked as cobblers or at repairing bicycle punctures. The 'love jihad' bogey is integrally tied to the myth that Muslims marry Hindu women to increase the population of Muslims.[36]

Modi's 'population control' campaign is likely to be another pretext to brand Muslims as unpatriotic and encourage discrimination and violence against them.

The Microfinance and SHG 'Revolution'

During the Noughties, governments in India began to push microfinance as a panacea for women's empowerment and poverty alleviation, in keeping with the neoliberal model of development. Surely, you will ask, microfinance institutions (MFIs) and self-help groups (SHGs) are doing the right thing by giving women affordable loans and financial empowerment and independence? That's what we've been told for decades.

The touchstone by which any policy for women should be judged is: does it challenge and dislodge unequal and oppressive power structures and ideologies, or strengthen them? As we've seen, policies against sex-selective abortion and open defecation have tended to strengthen rather than challenge such structures and ideologies. The same is true of MFIs and SHGs as well.

The neoliberal model sidelines any structural critiques of the economy or social relations (class, gender, caste and so on). Instead, it suggests that the rational 'choices' of individual women, based on individual self-interest, could empower them—not despite but *due* to their tendency to 'conform to gendered expectations or collude in the oppression of other women'.[37]

The microfinance model appropriated the feminist idea of collective action—ridding it, however, of solidarity and instead framing women as individual entrepreneurs who would discipline and police each other. While appropriating the feminist vocabulary of 'choice' and 'agency', the MFIs and SHGs drew upon, reinforced and even celebrated women's subjugation to unequal and oppressive patriarchal structures, arguing that this subjugation made them better borrowers.[38]

The hype around MFIs got a rude shock when fifty women committed suicide after being harassed, publicly shamed and hounded by MFI loan-recovery agents in 2010.[39] That's when the skeletons came tumbling out of the MFI closets. The MFIs charged exploitative rates of interest and resorted to humiliating and violent recovery methods in the style of moneylenders. Each suicide case was found to be linked to severe harassment by the companies in the name of loan recovery. Some were forced into prostitution to pay back their loans and many had to flee their houses and leave all their belongings behind.

A government study even found:

> Some MFI agents themselves are encouraging the debtors to commit suicide so that their loans are repaid. This happens because the borrowers are covered by insurance . . . The MFIs draw up an insurance cover for the borrower at the time of loan disbursement. In the eventuality of suicide, they recover the amount under the Loan Protection Fund (LPF) by which 10 per cent of the loan amount is deposited with the RBI, which repays the remaining loan amount due from the defaulter.[40]

The coercive and exploitative behaviour of the MFIs should have been no surprise: CEOs of MFIs made no secret of the fact that they saw the poor as lazy and unproductive, needing coercion to keep them disciplined and productive. This is starkly illustrated by the example of Vikram Akula, the CEO of SKS Microfinance, one of the MFIs that enjoyed the greatest penetration in the rural districts of Andhra Pradesh in 2010 and was implicated in many of the suicides. SKS followed the typical MFI trajectory: beginning as a 'not-for-profit' unit using grants and metamorphosing into a for-profit non-banking financial company (NBFC). In 2006, Akula figured on the *Time*'s list of the world's 100 most influential people, along with Nobel Prize winner Muhammad Yunus, and was awarded the Social Entrepreneur of the Year Award by Sonia Gandhi.[41] In 2010, SKS became the first MFI in Asia to go for an IPO listing on the stock market, attracting a record Rs 1600 crore, with a 5.8 million loan base, mainly among rural women in Andhra Pradesh, and a loan recovery rate of over 99 per cent.[42]

SKS recorded a spectacular increase in profits—from Rs 2 crore in 2008 to Rs 174 crore in 2010. Many of the people who committed suicides in Andhra Pradesh were SKS borrowers. SKS's phenomenal IPO listing provided affirmation that the business could assure its shareholders of reaping fat profits through 'double bottom line returns'. They made sure that the women in SHGs policed each other in paying their weekly instalments, forcing them to take responsibility for each other's payments. The company made an easy killing of 30 per cent interest on all loans. (Many MFIs took up to 60 per cent from the women by adding various other fines and figures for which they did not account.)

Akula and other MFIs claimed that while many of the people who committed suicides were MFI borrowers, it was their debts to traditional moneylenders and not SKS that led to the suicides. What can we make of that claim? Akula's book—*A Fistful of Rice: My Unexpected Quest to End Poverty through Profitability*—gives us a clue.[43] Akula says in the book that he modelled SKS on Walmart and McDonald's. The book indicated the weapons of public humiliation and shame deployed by SKS to recover loans:

When we started . . . people decided to test us by not paying . . . We instructed our loan officers not to leave . . . until the repayment came . . . The entire village would realize there was some issue . . . And that person would lose *izzath*—lose face. Losing face is a fairly devastating thing in a village context, and people will do anything to avoid it.[44]

The book also tells of an instance where a woman took a loan to buy a goat but used it to buy food. Akula's assistant told the woman: 'Buying food doesn't generate income, so you'll be no closer to getting out of poverty that way. Either buy a new goat or give us back the loan money.'[45] Buying food to address hunger was unprofitable and unproductive from the point of view of SKS. In such circumstances, where a woman is being humiliated for her inability to pay back a loan, or where she is being pressurized to return a loan that was used for consumption rather than for investment, she is forced to take more loans—often from traditional moneylenders—to pay back the MFIs. As she borrows from Peter to pay Paul, she is drawn deeper and deeper into the debt trap and is finally pushed to suicide.

It's important to remember this devastating experience now as MFIs once again attempt a comeback in India, bringing distress and suicides in their wake. In June 2015, two women, Namita and Sita, from Purshottampur village near Varanasi in UP, committed suicide because they were unable to repay loans they had taken from seven MFIs. Several other women in UP villages have fled to escape the MFI debt trap.[46] After the demonetization of Rs 500 and Rs 1000 currency notes by the Modi government in 2016, several women in Karnataka found themselves contemplating suicide, unable to repay loans taken from MFIs. One woman said, 'The representatives of the microfinance institutions verbally abuse us if we are not able to pay the instalments.'[47] Women have not taken this lying down; in 2017 they held protests against the abuse and harassment by MFI loan-recovery agents.[48] In 2016, women in four districts of the Vidarbha region of Maharashtra protested against coercive recovery practices of MFIs.[49]

In 2013, the then Union minister for rural development Jairam Ramesh admitted that microfinance had failed and was 'not the miracle it was touted to be'.[50] Ramesh contrasted the MFI model with the SHG one, saying that the bank-linked SHG model was a successful Indian innovation in microfinance.

But studies of SHGs have shown that they, too, are ridden with many of the same problems as MFIs: most notably, a tendency to instrumentalize and exploit the structural disempowerment of women, rather than 'empower' women to fight oppression and inequality. A study by the feminist organization Nirantar in 2007 found that for SHGs, as for MFIs, 'it is not the interests of women but their vulnerability that makes them attractive loan-takers'.[51] So, senior district bureaucrats in Gujarat explained that women make good debtors because, unlike men, who 'may disappear for days', 'women can't go anywhere, they can be located easily—they cannot run away, leaving their homes; they can be persuaded to repay easily as they feel shame more quickly and consider non-repayment as a betrayal of family honour'. The Nirantar study found that the SHGs were using 'existing gendered norms relating to a sense of shame and honour' to create peer pressure on women to repay loans.[52]

We have seen in previous chapters how women's lack of mobility, their confinement to the home and community, and notions of 'family honour' are at the root of much violence that women in India face. If this very vulnerability is what makes women attractive clients for SHGs and MFIs, how can the latter 'empower' women?

Women members of SHGs were not encouraged to take up issues of gender discrimination, unequal division of labour or violence in their households. Instead, as their labour for the SHG projects, which includes 'free labour for implementation or monitoring of government services', increases, they bear the dual burden of household work as well. Yet, government officials monitoring SHG schemes perpetuate the myth that women usually 'sit idle at home' or 'sleep in the houses idly' and SHGs provide them with work 'so they too can contribute to their families'![53] The official in charge of monitoring and evaluation of the World Bank-funded Swashakti SHG network vehemently opposed including any discussion of women's unequal social and economic status, saying, 'If we start teaching those things then our whole society will collapse and we will have no values and culture [left]. Whatever we do it should not destroy our family system.'[54]

The study observed:

> In all of the articulations related to the benefits of SHGs . . . women are being more and more closely identified with the institution of the family. This overwhelming focus on the family undermines the idea of a woman as an entity, with rights, interests and needs, which the women's movement has long been struggling for.[55]

The SHGs do not encourage women to recognize and collectively resist the structures of class, caste and gender and challenge the patriarchal notions of the 'good woman'. Instead, they 'harmonize traditional forms of gendered socialization with new forms of what it means to be a "good woman" in a neo-liberal economic framework'.[56] As a result, the SHGs tacitly impose dress codes on women, shaming women who chew paan, dress in old cotton saris rather than polyester ones, or do not oil and tightly braid their hair. Inevitably, it is women from Dalit and poorer households who are marginalized in the process. Further, instead of creating collectives and solidarities that break the caste barriers, SHGs tend to create caste-based groupings that are more effective to create peer pressure for loan recovery.

The Nirantar survey also found that while state governments, banks and corporations were benefiting hugely from the SHG networks, the SHGs were failing women on the very reason for their existence: providing credit to women. The survey found that '90 per cent of the

SHGs that save deposit their savings in banks. However, only 42 per cent of groups have received credit from banks.'[57] So governments, through SHGs, help financial institutions expand their credit base in rural areas, roping in poor women in their net, while claiming to usher in 'development' and women's 'empowerment'.

The SHGs and MFIs that are at worst exploitative and at best unhelpful are used by the state as their alibi to evade all accountability to implement 'programmatic or policy-level changes' to 'empower' women and reduce poverty. The state uses SHGs 'to project itself as the promoter of development while increasingly passing the onus of development to the poor, based on their own resources'.[58]

We've seen how the schemes and campaigns led by the state, the World Bank and other funding institutions not only avoid supporting women's assertion and autonomy, they, instead, leverage women's *lack of autonomy and mobility*. In Hindi, there is a saying, *'Jis laung se bhoot bhaga rahe the, bhoot usi laung mein tha'* (You were trying to exorcise the ghost with a clove, but the ghost was hiding in that very same clove)! The very same schemes and campaigns that are touted as 'empowering' the poor and deprived women deliberately reinforce patriarchal ideologies and structures. We're told that various desirable outcomes justify these anti-feminist means; but, as we've seen, this is far from true.

Is there an alternative? I believe there is. We need to recognize, first, that there's no 'smart' shortcut that can 'fix' women's problems. Feminist movements that fight to transform the *entire* system, with all its oppressive and exploitative social and economic structures, are genuinely empowering, because they build solidarity and collective strength that give individual women the confidence to fight for their rights. These movements that fight the system aren't 'negative' as our rulers claim: on the contrary they're the most hopeful and positive forces we have, because they believe that inequality and oppression can and must go, and they invest their time and energy in creating this change. Women who join these movements experience real, tangible changes in their everyday lives. Whether it's an abusive husband or an exploitative boss or landlord, they know they aren't alone in facing troubles. Solidarity is truly the only way for women to feel empowered and strong. Market-led 'smart' schemes that isolate women and force them to compete with and police each other disempower women.

As part of these movements, we need to hold governments accountable and make sure they don't wriggle off the hook. We need to demand government investment—in rations, in drinking water and sanitation, in public and household toilets, in fuel, in affordable and good-quality government schooling and colleges, in public health, in wages for women workers (such as ASHA, anganwadi and midday meal and SHG workers who subsidize government schemes with their free labour), and in ensuring more courts and judges, so that criminal and civil cases can move faster. Periodically, Indians get angry about how women are treated in India—and rightly so. But the problem is that the governments are easily able to divert that anger into demands for the death penalty for rapists in some cases that are fortunate enough to receive media attention. It costs governments nothing at all to echo and amplify those demands: we think we've won, and they continue to short-change women, slashing funding for public health and education, and for schemes for women. They let big corporate honchos (the Vijay Mallyas and the Nirav Modis) run away with lakhs of crores of people's hard-earned savings, while men and women who are unable to repay 'micro' loans are hounded to suicide. We need to stop letting governments get away with this trick—we need to make them put money (remember, it's *our* money) where their mouth is, and prioritize what women's movements demand.

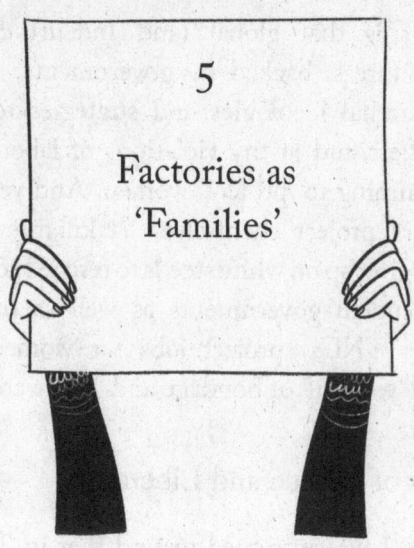

5

Factories as 'Families'

Families, households and organizations like khap panchayats are hostile to women's autonomy—but modern workplaces, connected to the globalized market, enable women to assert their economic and social freedom. Right?

Wrong.

It is hard to get much attention for the systemic, daily violence in such workplaces in the mainstream media. A khap panchayat that announces a 'ban' on mobile phones for women might make it to primetime TV news, where panellists shame them for holding back modernity and progress. But have you ever heard a similar discussion on television of corporations or a factory that bans mobile phones for women? Have you even heard of factories doing so?

The fact is that global (and Indian) corporations and manufacturers, backed by governments, deliberately deploy patriarchal ideologies and strategies to discipline women workers and justify violations of labour laws—all the while claiming to 'protect' women. And yet, the same manufacturers project themselves as knights in shining armour, charging up on white steeds to rescue Indian women in distress! Indian governments as well as transnational corporations (TNCs) project jobs for women in TNC factories as a 'way out' of bondage and 'backwardness'.

Fairy Tales of Rescue and Liberation

For instance, I was intrigued to find that in 2012, nearly identical 'news' stories appeared in several international print media outlets about the lingerie brand Victoria's Secret providing jobs to lift Indian women out of poverty. These stories, some of which appeared under bylines of journalists, were less like columns or reports and more like press releases or advertisements for the lingerie company.

It's worth taking a close look at one such story published by Reuters:

> Indian villager Jaya places the bright pink, sequined, moulded C-cupped designer bra under the needle of her sewing machine and carefully stitches the seams together.
>
> The padded 'Very Sexy' push-up bra which 22-year-old Jaya sews is for American lingerie retailer Victoria's Secret—designed to give a 'boost' to buyers in

hundreds of high-fashion boutiques across the United States. But a world away in this traditional rice-growing region of southern India, these luxurious bras are—in a different way—enhancing the lives of poor rural women.

'I knew nothing but the village before,' says Jaya. 'My parents just wanted me married as quickly as possible. They never saw me as an asset, just a burden . . .'

For conservative India's rural women—lucky to finish school, married before eighteen and confined to their villages—a project giving them jobs in the manufacturing sector is not just an end to poverty, but brings empowerment and respect in this deeply patriarchal society.

Located 30 km (18 miles) south of Chennai, Intimate Fashions—which also produces bras for Victoria's Secret brand 'Pink' and the La Senza brand—is one of thousands of firms that have set up in Tamil Nadu's Kanchipuram district in recent years.

Investment-friendly policies, close proximity to one of India's largest ports and an international airport, and easy access to a large, semi-literate workforce has helped make the area one of the most industrialized in the country.[1]

The story, by contrasting the words 'sexy' and 'bra' with 'semi-literate', 'poor', 'rural women' and 'deeply patriarchal society', and with an accompanying photograph of a dark-skinned woman worker working at a sewing machine to produce a pink bra, creates a seductive image for consumers in the West. The story plays on the word 'boost', suggesting that bras that push up or boost the bustline of women in the West can also boost the fortunes of poor women in rural India and push them up out of poverty and oppression. The message is that sexy lingerie consumed by women in the West can be liberating for the poor rural semi-literate women manufacturing them.

The same story goes on, however, to reveal certain telling facts about whose fortunes are getting a boost thanks to the availability of a cheap female workforce from rural India. Prasad Narayan Rege, general manager of Intimate Fashions, which employs Jaya among its 2500, mostly female, workers, is quoted explaining:

> Thousands of companies have mushroomed here, and there has been increasing competition to get good employees . . . so when the World Bank and the Tamil Nadu government came to us with the idea of employing women from some of the poorest communities and give them training, we saw a good opportunity. If it wasn't for this project, we would be in big trouble.[2]

If it were not for the World Bank and the Tamil Nadu government scheme providing 'good employees' (read 'docile employees') to the companies, the latter 'would be in big trouble'.

The story claims that the companies use 'culturally sensitive' recruitment practices:

> Under the Pudhu Vaazhvu (meaning 'New Life' in Tamil) project, funded by a US$350-million loan from

the World Bank . . . Firms are . . . in particular focusing
on recruiting young female employees. But this is not so
easy in these male-dominated communities . . . Officials
say firms have to adopt "culturally sensitive" approaches
such as bringing parents to see their manufacturing units
to show them the environment their daughters will be
working and living in as some girls must stay in hostels
set up by employers . . . But now, these young women are
breadwinners. Not only that, we are seeing positive social
changes taking place due to these jobs. Girls who were
married off straight out of school are now delaying their
marriages by three or four years.[3]

But behind the 'rescue narrative' reproduced in such
advertisements/news stories is a dirty 'secret': companies
like Victoria's Secret employed women under what used to
be called the 'Sumangali scheme', where children and young
girls worked for three years to earn their dowry as a 'lump
sum' amount.[4] The Sumangali scheme was withdrawn after
bad press about bonded labour and child labour, but many
studies have documented how the exploitative practices and
virtual bondage continue in the garment and textile factories
producing for global brands. And the exploitative practices
that enable and produce the bondage are disguised and
legitimized as none other than 'culturally sensitive practices'!

The Reuters story, and all the other identical or similar
stories appearing under various bylines in 2012 and since,[5]
reproduce colonial notions of 'rescuing' and 'saving brown
women' even as they give patriarchal surveillance a glossy
shining makeover.

'Culture' as Cover for Exploitation

In the garment and textile factories of Tamil Nadu and Karnataka, where there is a considerably large female workforce, studies document how managements invoke patriarchal notions of 'culture' and morality, and methods of public shaming and sexualized abuse to restrict women workers' mobility and access to means of communication, and thus deter and prevent women workers from unionizing.

A study of textile factories in Tamil Nadu titled 'Flawed Fabrics',[6] exposes a range of exploitative labour practices, including child labour and bonded labour as well as a range of gendered disciplinary measures for women workers. The mills are part of the supply chains for major European and American clothing brands. The hostels for the women workers, which are usually located on the factory grounds, severely restrict autonomy and mobility. Staying in the factory hostel is compulsory for workers who migrate from other districts or villages. 'Flawed Fabrics' found that:

> At all five investigated mills . . . workers are not allowed to leave the hostel on their own. There is hardly any outside contact . . . Workers may only contact their parents through the hostel phone. Mobile phones are not allowed and after-work activities are limited. Under the pretext of cultural traditions, girls and women are effectively locked up.[7]

We saw in the third chapter how households and social and political groups confiscate mobile phones and surveil communications of women in the name of protecting them from 'love jihad'. These globalized factories use the same methods:

> If workers want to make a phone call, the warden will check the number they are dialling. The workers may only contact their parents if their number has been given to the warden. Phone calls are always made in the presence of the hostel warden . . . The warden will check the girl workers; where they are going, which shift they are doing.[8]

The things the women workers are scolded for include talking to co-workers (all mills), and talking to male workers (at the Premier, Super and Sulochana mills).[9]

Studies of the neighbouring state of Karnataka also document similar work conditions. 'Production of Torture: A Study on Working Conditions Including Work Place Harassments Facing Women Garment Workers in Bangalore and Other Districts', a report by civil liberties and feminist organizations (PUCL, et al), found that here, too, women were prevented from communicating with the outside world: 'Once workers enter the factories, they are required to be cut off from all contact with the external world, even in case of emergencies.'[10] The report found that banning workers from carrying mobile phones in the workplace was widespread.

> Upon a violation of the rule, some confiscate the mobile phone, others impose a fine, and some others compel the worker to give a written apology and guarantee

that she will henceforth not carry the phone into the workplace. Many workers surreptitiously carry their phones into the factory and keep them on a silent mode, as they wish to be contacted at a time of emergency.[11]

As in the Tamil Nadu factories, workers are prohibited from talking to each other:

> Since the shop floors are arranged one behind another, it prevents any form of interaction between the workers except during the 15-20 minutes' lunch break—this prevents any form of cohesion among the workers . . . When not being present at the work stations, workers are consistently questioned about their whereabouts. Even toilet and canteen visits are monitored by security.[12]

Like those used by university and college administrations to justify discriminatory hostel rules for women students, arguments used by the factory management invoke 'culture' and parental concerns about 'safety and security'. For example, responding to a draft version of the 'Flawed Fabrics' report, the management of Sulochana mill wrote:

> [Because] of our state Tamil Nadu culture and the expectation of girls' parents, they have been provided accommodation in the hostel of the management. Only for safety and security, the parents and girls decided to stay in the hostel and come for work.[13]

These studies also offer insights into how women themselves can internalize patriarchal ideologies of 'culture' and morality. The report describes how women workers, while resenting the 'prison-like' conditions, also subscribe to the idea that such restrictions are to be expected for Indian women:

> In rural Tamil Nadu, it is generally felt that it is not safe for young unmarried women to stay on their own, in a place where there are no parents, relatives or community members to keep an eye on them. As one of the workers at the Premier mill put it: 'We are girls; we must follow some values in society.'[14]

Humiliation and Harassment as Disciplinary Methods

Studies from both Tamil Nadu and Karnataka document the extreme emotional distress to which women garment workers are subjected. The demeaning, exhausting and exploitative conditions of work, which, in some cases, include humiliating corporal punishments, have made some women workers suicidal.

The 'Flawed Fabrics' report records an attempted suicide by a seventeen-year-old worker at Best Corporation's spinning mill in Dharapuram, one of the units investigated, which was reported in Tamil newspapers on 12 October 2013. The young woman attempted suicide after she was 'scolded and hit in front of the other workers because she had used a cell phone inside the spinning mill' and 'charged a Rs 500 penalty and was forced to clean the wall where the workers spit out'. She could leave the factory premises only after the intervention of a trade union.[15]

The report from Karnataka also documents how women workers are subjected to continuous surveillance and humiliating corporal punishments to pressurize them to meet production targets. The punishments include:

> Being scolded in public at the shop floor in the presence of all other workers, or through the public address system . . . Forcibly switching off the machine and being compelled to stand at the shop floor for long in front of other workers . . . Being made to stand outside the work place/gate of the factory for a long period of time for taking leave without prior permission or for reporting for work a few minutes late; When a woman garment worker goes to the toilet, sending someone to follow her to ensure that she does not waste time.[16]

The PUCL report documents how 'male supervisors, floor in-charges, including managers, call the women workers by abusive names . . . and cast aspersions on their character'. Such 'scolding' includes asking the woman worker 'if she ate food or shit, whether she is a woman who lives on the streets, and asking her why she was late to work' and so on to suggest that she is a sex worker.[17] Such abuse draws on forms of humiliation that are shaped by caste and gender. Cleaning or touching human excreta is associated with the oppressed Dalit castes and forcing people to 'eat shit' is a common caste atrocity to which Dalits are subjected. This particular abuse amounts to caste atrocity against a woman worker if she is a Dalit and can also be experienced as demeaning and humiliating by a woman who is not a Dalit. Saying that a

woman belongs 'on the streets' suggests she is a sex worker—
to call a woman a sex worker is to slut-shame her.

The punishments and 'scoldings' are designed to be
exemplary: their public, performative character enables
them to be used to discipline, demoralize and control the
entire body of workers, not just the individual worker who
is being chastised. The report observes:

> A worker is sometimes made to stand aside for an hour
> as punishment before the assembly. This often reduces
> the humiliated worker to tears. Equally, this isolation of
> worker from the assembly of the workers, who look on
> helplessly and silently, makes all of them feel lost and
> incapacitated.[18]

Women in the Karnataka factories are frequently subjected
to physical violence, 'including throwing the garment at the
worker's face [most frequently reported by the workers],
hitting the woman worker on her back, dragging her out
from her workstation, and physically compelling her to stand
away from it'. Sexual harassment is also common, including
'staring hard at a woman worker in a sexual manner;
making obscene threats, such as saying that chilli powder
will be applied on the woman's vagina if she does not work
efficiently'; as well as 'scolding' using sexual expletives.[19]

In the globalized workplace, then, surveillance,
sexualized abuse, sexual harassment and public humiliation
are not aberrations—these are *integral* to the production
process, and are used to keep the women workers insecure
by pressurizing them to meet impossible production targets.

The PUCL report notes how the systemic harassment at work keeps women in an emotionally fraught state, given to frequent bouts of weeping, depression, suicidal thoughts, suicide attempts and humiliation at the social shaming associated with garment work.

The workplace harassment also strains family relationships. The women workers do a 'double shift', that is, bear the entire social reproductive burden[20]: 'caring for children/aged people in the family, cooking/cleaning and running the house are solely her responsibilities'. While their husbands or in-laws 'do not object to her work', they 'are nasty when she is late or is unable to complete household work'. The social reproductive burden of providing emotional support is also largely borne by women rather than by men; as a result, 'most women garment workers expressed an inability to share such feelings [of depression, job-related stress, etc.] with their husbands, as they feared that the husband would compel the woman to leave the job, which she desperately needs to financially support her family'.[21]

Moral Shaming to Deter Solidarity

The reports from both Tamil Nadu and Karnataka indicate the systematic way in which the garment industry uses the precariousness and vulnerability of women to exploit them financially and 'fashion a more disciplined and hence cheaper workforce of women'.[22] Women's vulnerability to suggestions of sexual immorality helps deter their mutual solidarity—in communities as well as in factories, women are expected and encouraged to maintain a distance from the 'immoral' women, and to strive to prove they are 'respectable, good women' by their willing submission to regimes of surveillance and restrictions on mobility and means of communication.

In the Tamil Nadu factories, the women workers are younger and unmarried—and in their case, factories draw on parents' anxieties about dowry payment as well as about preventing daughters from contracting 'unwanted/ undesirable' (read 'in violation of caste and community boundaries') romantic/sexual relationships to justify their incarceration in hostels.

The women workers in the Karnataka factories tend to be older, married women. In their case, sexualized shaming tactics also help deter them from seeking support from husbands or in-laws. The abusive conditions of work at the place of production (the factories) strain the conditions of life and social relationships at the site of social reproduction (the households). Likewise, women's vulnerability to or fear of violence or humiliation in their own households, and the pressures of having to earn to support economically precarious families, make them more likely to submit without complaint to the abusive disciplinary regimes at work.

Though the rationalizations for gendered restrictions on the freedom of women workers invoke concerns of 'culture' and 'safety', the fact is that these restrictions have the immensely practical value of deterring unionization. By preventing women workers from interacting with male workers or activists from outside and discouraging socialization even among women workers on the factory floor, they are effectively prevented from even visualizing the possibility of unionizing.

The 'Flawed Fabrics' report notes that the right to association and the right to collective bargaining, though recognized in India's labour laws, are widely violated in the garment factories.[23] Interviews with workers in the report illustrate how the gendered restrictions on them make it difficult for them to consider joining a union:

> We have no outside contact so how could we ever join a trade union? . . . I am a female worker then how can I become a member of trade union? . . . I don't think that the workers are having much freedom of joining the trade union because all the workers here are girls.[24]

The fact that unions, far from being able to recruit women workers as members, are prevented even from meeting or interacting with them, means that exploitative practices in the Tamil Nadu factories are able to continue unchallenged. The 'Flawed Fabrics' report also establishes that the infamous Sumangali scheme—which subjects women workers to bonded labour on the pretext that they will earn their own dowry in the form of a lump-sum payment—continues undeterred by the fact that the scheme stands officially abandoned.[25]

In many cases, employers fail to transfer the required amount to the provident fund or cite various minor infractions on the part of the worker to deny them due payment. Such practices are illegal—which is why the Sumangali scheme is no longer formally in effect—and yet they are rampant.

A Global Phenomenon

Globalized workplaces across Asia, not just in India, draw on familial patriarchal norms and moral regimes to discipline women workers. These gendered forms of discipline and surveillance infantilize women workers and place managements 'in loco parentis', or in the place of parents. Melissa Wright documents and analyses similar forms of discipline invoked by Chinese managers of multinational factories in China.[26] She notes that while both male and female workers were expected to live in dormitories, female workers were 'forbidden from leaving the building at any time and on any day except for Sunday' while the male workers 'walked between the two facilities on a regular basis'. Male workers 'took breaks outside the doors, where they would smoke cigarettes and talk until a manager walked through, when they would head inside'. The gendered explanations offered by Chinese managers for the stricter control on women workers are similar to those offered by managements of Indian factories; they describe their roles 'as those of a parent with an unpredictable teenage girl who requires a strong patriarchal hand to keep her under control'.[27] One manager said 'that his own knowledge of Chinese culture and his own experience as a father meant that he was particularly suited for his job as production manager over a young female Chinese labor force.'[28]

The Chinese raise their daughters to be very obedient . . .
The family is strict, more strict than in America . . . The
girls, sometimes, do not know what to do when they move

away from their family. They can lose their obedience. They are naïve. I have two daughters, and we are very strict with them. Chinese daughters are good daughters, but you have to protect them from dangerous things in the city.[29]

The gendered methods of disciplining women garment workers in Bangladesh, as described by Dina Siddiqi, have striking parallels with the methods we have discussed in Indian contexts. Siddiqi observes:

[The women workers are regulated] through a distinct moral regime, separating the 'good' girls from the 'immoral' ones. A highly sexualized regime of verbal discipline, as well as more overt forms of sexual harassment, also serves to keep women in their place. In this universe, the good woman is the good worker—those who are morally disciplined; that is, those who do not protest or draw too much attention to themselves—are deserving of managerial protection. Those who challenge such norms are much more vulnerable to managerial sexual advances.[30]

As in the Karnataka factories, sexualized abuse—such as hurling insults that question the morality of the worker's father or mother—are common in Bangladeshi factories.

Such practices are found even in other locations where women are part of the globalized workforce. One such instance can be found in the export processing zone of the Dominican Republic, as outlined in a study that enquires into the deployment of practices of sexual harassment to keep women from organizing.[31]

Relying on Women's Unpaid Work

Patriarchal ideologies and methods, which draw on assumptions that a woman's place is in the home and that domestic labour is not 'work', have come in very handy when exploiting women workers and invisibilizing their labour.

In the liberalization decades since the 1990s, much of the 'increase' in women's employment has been in 'self-employment' rather than in paid work. The phrase 'self-employed' is highly misleading, suggesting that the woman has control over her work and is free from the exploitation associated with, say, work in a factory or a field.

The truth is that 'self-employed' more often than not means 'self-exploited', where women workers have to ensure a do-it-yourself home-based exploitative routine to serve their employers' interests. Home-based subcontracting or 'putting out' is increasingly being resorted to by manufacturers internationally. The reason is that the workers thus employed (very often women and children) are out of the protection of labour laws and trade unions. Economist Jayati Ghosh notes that the increase in women's self-employment in India, in large part, is 'a distress-driven phenomenon, led by the inability to find adequately gainful paid work'.[32]

The title of Ghosh's book, *Never Done and Poorly Paid*, refers, appropriately, to the expression that 'women's work is never done': that is, domestic labour is never-ending and unpaid to boot. And nowhere is this title more appropriate than in the context of the government scheme workers.

The World Bank-supported Integrated Child Development Scheme (ICDS) is supposed to be India's answer to the country's appalling hunger, malnutrition and mortality indicators among women and children. The entire scheme rests on the anganwadi workers and helpers—one of each is allotted to an anganwadi centre, which is supposed to cater to a population of 1000 (and 700 in tribal areas). Despite the Supreme Court's repeated instructions, the government is yet to expand the scheme to provide universal coverage. An enormous burden of work rests on the shoulders of the only two women functionaries at each centre—providing nutrition, immunization and basic health check-ups, antenatal and postnatal care to children and expectant mothers as well as the care of newborns and small children, nutrition and health education to womens, referral of cases of malnutrition and illnesses to hospitals, and even daily non-formal preschool education to children between three and five years of age. In addition, due to their dedication, other government schemes and initiatives also come to routinely rest on them—total literacy, election duties, awareness- and health-related campaigns and so on. Yet, they are not treated on a par with other government employees, and called 'social workers' or 'voluntary workers', who are not paid wages!

It is much the same case with the ASHAs (Accredited Social Health Activists) who are the backbone of the National Rural Health Mission (NRHM). They have a mind-boggling range of seemingly endless duties, yet they are called 'honorary volunteers' as a pretext to underpay and deny them rights. The NRHM mission statement says that the ASHA will be a health activist responsible for creating awareness in the community on health issues, a promoter of good health practices, and 'will also provide a minimum package of curative care . . . and make timely referrals'. Sounds like a lot of work? Well, as Ghosh observes, NRHM piles on a whole lot more on the ASHAs' shoulders: they must create awareness on nutrition, sanitation and hygiene; counsel women on birth-preparedness, safe delivery, breastfeeding, contraception, prevention of common infections and care of young children; facilitate access to immunization, antenatal and postnatal check-ups, ICDS, sanitation, etc.; arrange to escort pregnant women and children requiring treatment and/or admission to the nearest health facility; provide medical care for minor ailments such as diarrhoea, fever, first aid and TB treatment; provide ORS, iron and folic acid tablets, chloroquine, disposable delivery kits, oral contraceptive pills and condoms; inform health authorities at primary health centres or sub-centres about births and deaths and the outbreak of diseases; promote the construction of household toilets; and work with gram panchayats to develop a comprehensive village health plan. ASHAs (local women with at least eight years of schooling) are expected to do all of the above skilled work with just twenty-three days of training!

ASHAs work eight hours on normal days—and, of course, since deliveries and sicknesses do not follow any set time schedule and tend to come unannounced at all odd hours of day or night, the ASHA is on call 24*7.

Ghosh adds:

> And, then, amazingly, the proposed remuneration for
> this woman worker is—nothing at all! The NRHM
> envisages that the 'ASHA would be an *honorary volunteer*
> and would not receive any salary or honorarium'.
> State governments pay a miserly 'incentive' amount of
> Rs 500—which women in some states have through
> struggles managed to increase to Rs 1000–1500 per month.

Exactly as the women's work in the home is famously 'never
done and unpaid', the work of the women employed in the
anganwadi, ASHA and midday-meal schemes is 'never done
and poorly paid'. It is indeed a shame that major large-scale
government programmes have been 'designed and launched
by explicitly relying on the unpaid labour of women', to
provide essential public services, 'trading on the time-worn
stereotype of caring women who serve their families and
communities selflessly without any thought of return'.[33]

The case of another flagship government scheme,
the Sarva Shiksha Abhiyan (SSA), also World Bank-
supported, is a comment both on the state of women in
public employment as well as on the substandard schooling
being passed off as the World Bank–approved model of
'parallel primary schooling' in India. SSA teachers, a very
large number of which are women, usually have some
schooling (Class VIII or more) but no pedagogical training.
Their monthly wages are as low as Rs 1000–3000. Such
teachers constitute nearly 16 per cent of all school 'teachers'
in the country!

The Political Economy of 'Familyism'

The organized attacks on women's autonomy (in the name of curbing 'love jihad' or 'protecting women') by Sangh outfits and caste bodies are often portrayed by the media as being at odds with the Government of India's proclaimed aim of promoting corporate-led 'development'. We may reassure ourselves with this imagined contradiction, but it is little more than a piece of fiction. In reality, as we have seen above, corporations, manufacturers and the forces of the globalized market are interested and invested in suppressing women's autonomy to create a docile workforce and to deter unionization. When it comes to appeasing corporates and weakening labour laws, most governments in India have been on the same page. The UPA government that ruled between 2004 and 2013 also battled unions in the attempt to erode protections offered by labour laws, and deter and punish unionization. Some of the most militant struggles of the Indian workers' movements have been fought to claim the right to unionize, such as the Honda workers' movement in Gurgaon–Manesar in 2005 and the Maruti Manesar workers' movement in 2011–12, which were met with severe and unrelenting repression by Congress regimes, both in Haryana and at the Centre.[34]

Since 2014, the Government of India led by the BJP has been inviting global corporations to come and 'Make in India', promising 'low-cost manufacturing'.[35] 'Low-cost manufacturing' demands low-cost labour. One of the ways in which this is achieved is by flouting labour laws and preventing workers from organizing and unionizing to seek implementation of those laws.

Why does a government that welcomes Indian and multinational corporations to 'Make in India' also patronize outfits that attack women's autonomy, especially in the matter of inter-caste and interfaith marriages?[36] This question ceases to puzzle when we see how an ideology of conservative paternalistic protectionism towards women (an ideology that is condoned by the Indian state and most Indian political formations but which achieves its most virulent form in the Sangh Parivar) has its uses in disciplining women's labour both in the spaces of social reproduction (households, communities, schools and colleges) and production.

The twin uses of this ideology become especially apparent when we look at how the image of 'family' and 'home' is deployed in the literature and propaganda of the BJP and its parent organization, the RSS.

The BJP manifesto for the 2014 Lok Sabha polls, in its section on labour reforms, declared:

> [We] propose to encourage industry owners and labour to embrace the concept of 'Industry Family'. This concept, in which industry owners and labours bond as a family, is guided by the principles of efficiency, skill development and upgradation, productivity, appropriate wages and perquisites, and security towards this end.

The 'family' metaphor for industrial management and labour relations is used to recast relations between workers and bosses as harmonious relations within the 'industry family', thus justifying erosion and dilution of the labour laws. The implications of this metaphor for women workers are obvious: the denial of autonomy to women in the name of 'protection' inside families is rendered 'natural' in factories as well.

The same metaphor serves the Sangh's efforts to legitimize other hierarchies too. The RSS often refers to its constellation of organizations as a 'parivar'—a family. The family metaphor is evoked by the RSS to valorize the patriarchal family and subjugation of women—even to the extent of justifying wife-beating as necessary chastisement of erring wives. The Rashtra Sevika Samiti cadres describe themselves as 'familyist not feminist';[37] feminist assertions of women's autonomy are painted as Western-inspired disruptions of the harmonious Indian family. Oppressive social practices are all rationalized as having evolved to 'protect' women from rapacious Muslims.[38]

Autonomy Should Not Be a Luxury

The RSS shares with the forces of corporate globalization a deep hostility to and fear of women's autonomy. Why do modern global corporations fear women's autonomy in their personal and sexual lives? They fear it because women's vulnerability in their personal lives contributes to their precariousness and exploitability at work; and moreover they recognize that such autonomy cannot remain hermetically sealed in personal spaces of family, household, caste and community—it is likely to leak into workspaces as well, spurring unionization and collective social and political action. A woman worker, for instance, may use her mobile phone and her freedom from surveillance at home and work to keep in contact with a male friend or lover from some other caste or community; and she may also use it to be in touch with her comrades, and to organize and attend union meetings and even to organize flash strikes, as garment workers of Karnataka have indeed done on more than one occasion!

That's why 'autonomy' is by no means an 'elite' concern. In fact, the notion that autonomy is only for urban-middle-class or upper-class women, while working-class women must only worry about bread-and-butter issues and gas cylinders, is elitist! It's no coincidence that women workers of the nineteenth and early twentieth centuries demanded 'bread and roses too': the right not only to subsistence and survival but to all the good things in life as well.

Think about what a campaign like Why Loiter?—which asserts the right of women to access the city for pleasure and leisure and not only for work—could mean for a Dalit woman sanitation worker. When sanitation workers of Bengaluru (*powrakarmika*s, which means municipal employees) went on strike on International Women's Day (8 March) 2017, demanding unpaid dues as well as a range of other rights, a journalist came up to ask Meena, a powrakarmika, what her demands were. Meena's teenage daughter, Monisha, was by her side, and interrupted her mother to tell the journalist, 'My mother has always wanted to visit Cubbon Park, I want her to get a weekly day off, so that I can take her to spend the day at the park!' The right to relax and loiter in the public parks, to watch a movie, to simply enjoy oneself is as much a basic right as food, education and health.

Noting that Article 24 of the Universal Declaration of Human Rights recognizes that 'everyone has the right to rest and leisure, including reasonable limitation of working hours and periodic holidays with pay', Kalpana Wilson points out:

> The question of the lack of time and leisure is a particularly important one for women agricultural labourers, who work extremely long hours both on the fields and in the household. The right to leisure time has been central to struggles of labour everywhere, but like economic rights in general, it is ignored in neoliberal 'rights-based' development discourse . . . Assumption that the time of women in poor households is infinitely elastic, and can always incorporate more income generating activity has come to be taken for granted in development discourse and policy, even when the notion of a double or triple burden (of productive, reproductive and community labour) is acknowledged. For example, a recent study of the conditions of women agricultural labourers in Orissa published by the state government, while noting that the women in the study worked for an average of 14–16 hours in the lean season, and more in the peak season, still insists that 'leisure time' income generating activities should be promoted among them, because currently leisure time is 'sometimes non-productive' involving 'gossiping, sleeping, playing cards and watching TV'!'[39]

A poster from the early-twentieth-century workers' struggle in the US for the eight-hour day declared that the twenty-four-hour day must be divided into three parts: eight hours each for work, rest and 'what we will' (whatever we like or enjoy). Of course, the capitalist employer wants to increase the 'work' part of the day as much as possible and shrink the 'rest' and 'leisure' part of the day as much as possible. Think about this twenty-four-hour day from the point of view of a woman. Even if a woman is not a paid worker, she is actually working twenty-four hours a day—because domestic labour has no fixed working hours: if a baby cries in the night or wets itself, it must be attended to immediately. Domestic labour involves collecting fuel and water as well as the actual process of cooking. It involves playing with children, making them do homework, wiping the tears of a crying child, waking up in the middle of the night to care for a baby, a sick child or a sick adult. If she is a paid worker, she is doing a double shift, because after a hard day at work, she still has to come home and cook and care for others. She does not have eight hours for rest and eight hours for 'what you will' (which can include leisure, enjoyment as well as attending meetings of unions and women's organizations). She has a much harder struggle than men to make time for these activities.

Challenging the gender division of labour at home by requiring men to bear a fair share of the burden of domestic labour, and demanding that the employer and the state bear greater burdens of social reproduction, by providing welfare measures, water, fuel, food, messes or canteens providing cooked food, pensions for the elderly, healthcare, maternity benefits, education and child care, transport, as well as paid weekly and festival holidays are all very much part of working-class struggles that assert women's rights to greater autonomy and leisure.

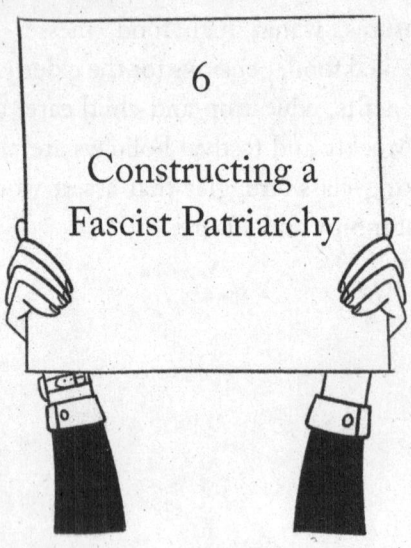

6

Constructing a
Fascist Patriarchy

Patriarchies produce a potentially hospitable space
where racism, casteism and communalism could meet.
—Kumkum Sangari[1]

The chronic lack of autonomy for women in India provides
a fertile ground for a variety of communal, casteist and
fascist political forces to breed. We've seen in previous
chapters how the RSS in India uses the bogey of 'love
jihad' to unleash an organized political attack on women's
autonomy, and use 'protection of women' as a pretext
for violence against Muslim men. Few political forces
(except the Left) in India have even paid lip service to, let

alone seriously promoted women's autonomy. By tacitly condoning attacks on women's autonomy (as, for instance, Congress governments have done in Haryana) these political forces have contributed to creating a patriarchal common sense that has stood fascists and communalists in good stead. But among political forces in India, it is the RSS and BJP alone that articulate an ideology and develop a practice that is explicitly, proudly patriarchal and hostile to women's autonomy. No other political force, for instance, organizes a countrywide network to track and attack interfaith relationships and marriages, or organizes yearly attacks on couples celebrating Valentine's Day.

Why bring in politics when speaking of women's rights, you may ask? Moreover, if one is talking about political parties and organizations, why single out the RSS and BJP?

It's true that all political parties in India can boast of gross misogyny by one or the other of its prominent leaders. Mulayam Singh Yadav of the Samajwadi Party said, 'Boys will be boys,' to trivialize rape, and also suggested that 'gang rape' was a physical impossibility.[2] Anil Basu of the CPI(M) compared Mamata Banerjee to the sex workers of Sonagachi, and Susanta Ghosh, another CPI(M) leader, took a dig at Banerjee's unmarried status at an election rally: 'Karo kopaley jodi lal na jotey, taholey tar lal dekhlei rag hoy' (A woman without the good fortune of bearing sindur [vermilion, the symbol of her marital status] on her forehead is bound to become infuriated if she so much as catches a glimpse of the colour red).[3] Banerjee referred to the rape at Park Street as a 'sajano ghotona' (cooked-up case) while her then Sports Minister Madan Mitra asked what the divorced mother of two children was doing at a nightclub so late at night.[4] The Social Democratic Party of India (SDPI), that spoke loudly about Hadiya's rights, issued death threats to a Christian man, Harison, who married a Muslim woman, Shahana, because they too see women as the property of a community.[5]

The misogyny displayed by all these parties and their leaders must, of course, be called out and held accountable. Political leaders should have to suffer electoral consequences—lose votes—for perpetuating rape culture, victim-blaming and misogyny.

What makes the BJP a 'party with a difference', however, is the ideological vision of its parent organization, the RSS. The RSS's goal is for India to become a Hindu Rashtra. What will be the place of women and sexual and gender minorities in that Hindu nation? What will be the position of religious minorities and oppressed castes in that Hindu nation? Seeking answers to these questions also gives us clues about where the RSS picked up the idea of branding love between Hindu women and Muslim men as 'love jihad'. Knowing the genealogies and lineages of today's political ideologies can also help us be better armed and better warned to avert repeating disasters that the world has experienced before.

Lineages of the 'Love Jihad' Bogey

In his autobiography *Mein Kampf*, Adolf Hitler accused Jewish men of seeking to deliberately 'pollute' the 'Aryan' race by seducing and encouraging black men to seduce, white 'Aryan' women:

The black-haired Jewish youth lies for hours in ambush, a Satanic joy in his face, for the unsuspecting girl whom he pollutes with his blood and steals from her own race. By every means, he seeks to wreck the racial bases of the nation he intends to subdue. Just as individually he deliberately befouls women and girls, so he never shrinks from breaking the barriers race has erected against foreign elements. It was, and is, the Jew who brought Negroes to the Rhine, brought them with the same aim and with deliberate intent to destroy the white race he hates, by persistent bastardization, to hurl it from the cultural and political heights it has attained, and to ascend to them as its masters. He deliberately seeks to lower the race level by steady corruption of the individual . . .[6]

Sounds familiar? In India, the 'love jihad' theory propagated by communal outfits claiming that Muslim men deliberately set out to seduce and 'steal' Hindu women as part of a 'jihadi' campaign shares many features with such an ideology.

One of the key aspects of Nazism—the racist ideology of Hitler's party that claimed superiority for the 'Aryan' (white German) race and unleashed atrocities and genocide on the Jews, gypsies and many other minorities—was the deterrence and prohibition of interracial relationships between men and women. Note how Hitler, in the passage quoted above, claims that Jewish young men steal unsuspecting Aryan girls 'from their own race'. He describes non-Jewish women as unsuspecting victims who are the property of 'their race' rather than women with control over their own minds and hearts. The RSS, in exactly the same way, claims that Hindu women who fall in love with Muslim men are 'girls' who cannot be trusted with decisions about their own lives, and who are moreover the property of the Hindu community.

Remember, Hitler and the Nazis, who viewed 'Aryan' women as racial property, regimented and repressed those same women as well. In a speech in September 1934, addressing the Nazi women's organization, Hitler said that the German woman's 'world is her husband, her family, her children, and her home'—something that was expressed in Nazi propaganda as the creed of the 'three Ks'—'*Küche, Kirche, Kinder*' (kitchen, church and children).[7]

In the same way, the RSS, that uses Hindu women as an excuse to unleash violence on Muslim men and women, is also, as we have seen, violent towards Hindu women, using torture to coerce them into giving up 'forbidden' interfaith relationships. RSS-affiliated women's organizations hold camps persuading their cadres to accept domestic violence as chastisement for 'misbehaviour'.[8]

Lynch Mobs to 'Protect Womanhood'?

If the RSS took Hitler's ideology as a model for its own, what did Hitler himself take for his inspiration and model? In 1934, leading Nazi lawyers met to draft the anti-Jewish 'Nuremberg Laws': they took for their model the notorious racist 'Jim Crow' laws of the US South.[9]

African American people, descended from slaves, won freedom in 1863. But between the American Civil War that ended in 1865 and World War II, an elaborate system of racist laws were enacted to ensure racial segregation, curtail the civil liberties of African American people, and prevent them from voting. These racist laws—known as 'Jim Crow' laws—were backed by thousands of lynchings. In the era of the 'Jim Crow' laws that criminalized interracial sexual relationships and marriages, African American men in the US were frequently killed for having or even being suspected of having consensual relationships with white women. Mob lynching of such men—often on the pretext of allegations of 'raping' white women—was extremely common. Photographs of these lynchings were widely sold and circulated, showing crowds of white people rejoicing around the bodies of black men who had been burnt alive or hanged by lynch mobs. In these photographs, it was common to see white men pointing at the body of the victim—the pointing finger was a warning to other African Americans that this would be their fate if they crossed the colour line.[10]

Ida B. Wells, one of the leading campaigners against lynching in the American South, pointed out in a celebrated speech that 'crimes against women is the excuse, not the cause' of the lynchings. Wells said:

> What is the cause of this awful slaughter? This question is answered almost daily—always the same shameless falsehood that 'Negroes are lynched to protect womanhood'. Standing before a Chautauqua assemblage, John Temple Graves, at once champion of lynching and apologist for lynchers, said: 'The mob stands today as the most potential bulwark between the women of the

South and such a carnival of crime as would infuriate the world and precipitate the annihilation of the Negro race.' This is the never-varying answer of lynchers and their apologists. All know that it is untrue. The cowardly lyncher revels in murder, then seeks to shield himself from public execration by claiming devotion to woman. But truth is mighty and the lynching record discloses the hypocrisy of the lyncher as well as his crime.[11]

The racist mob was not the saviour of women in the American South. And the communal mob is not a saviour of Hindu women in India. The former saw white women as racial property just as the communal mob sees Hindu women as community property.

The Sangh's Nazi and Racist Model

Just as Hitler and the Nazis took the Jim Crow laws of the US as an inspiration and a model, the RSS and its fellow travellers like the Hindu Mahasabha, in the 1930s and the 1940s, took both Nazism and American racism as inspiration and model for their Hindu nation.

RSS founder M.S. Golwalkar, for instance, wrote admiringly of 'German race pride' and Germany's purge of Jews as 'a good lesson for us in Hindusthan to learn and profit by'.[12] Golwalkar, embracing the Nazi model, wrote:

[Muslims and Christians] must either adopt the Hindu culture and language, must learn to respect and hold in reverence Hindu religion, must entertain no idea but

> those of the glorification of the Hindu race and culture,
> i.e., of the Hindu nation and must lose their separate
> existence to merge in the Hindu race, or may stay in
> the country, wholly subordinated to the Hindu nation,
> claiming nothing, deserving no privileges, far less any
> preferential treatment not even citizen's rights.[13]

V.D. Savarkar, too, in his presidential address to the twenty-second session of the Hindu Mahasabha at Madurai in 1940, spoke of how the 'touch of Nazi or Fascist magical wand' had proved a 'congenial tonic' for Germany's national health. Savarkar also spoke, in a 1944 interview with American war correspondent Tom Treanor, of how Muslims in India should be treated as 'Negroes' in America were.[14]

Fascism doesn't happen overnight. The concentration camps and the pogroms are the endpoint. Recognizing the hallmarks of creeping (or racing) fascism—racial/communal profiling, sexual demonization of the 'Other', daily targeted lynch-mob attacks and killings—is important.

'Women's Protection' as Pretext for Communal Violence

One of the many pretexts for the rash of lynch-mob violence and communal violence against Muslims in India has been the bogey of 'love jihad' or 'rape'. Do you recall seeing a photograph of a Sikh police officer, Gagandeep, rescuing a Muslim man from a violent mob in Uttarakhand?[15] I saw a video of the incident: the Muslim man was being attacked for walking in public with a Hindu woman. The mob attacked the woman too, threatening her: 'Going out with a Muslim? Cut her to pieces!'[16]

There have been many other such instances in UP, which remind us that Gagandeep's actions—which we ought to be able to expect from every police officer—are sadly rare. In September 2017, BJP Mahila Morcha's Aligarh leader, Sangeeta Varshney, was caught on camera slapping a Dalit woman *inside a police station* for being in a relationship with a Muslim man. Varshney said: '*Tujhe itni sharam bhi nahi hai, tu kya zyaada badi ho gayi? Tujhme itni bhi samajh nahi hai ki kaun Hindu hai kaun Musalman hai?* (Don't you have any shame, do you think you're that grown up? Can you not even understand who is a Hindu and who a Muslim?).' And the police booked the boyfriend for 'obscenity in a public place'—instead of booking Varshney for assault![17]

In Meerut on 23 September 2018, a VHP mob barged into a Muslim man's room, where a woman friend and classmate had come to study. The mob called the police—which, instead of arresting the mob members, took the man and woman into custody. They beat up the woman, saying, 'You're a Hindu and you want a Muslim?'[18] And they threatened the man with arrest. The police personnel were suspended briefly—and then, lo and behold, transferred a mere week later to the chief minister's own home constituency, Gorakhpur![19]

The Muzaffarnagar communal violence of 2013 and the resulting communal polarization played a huge role in mobilizing Hindu votes for the BJP in western UP.

Muslims were attacked after BJP leaders made provocative speeches claiming Muslim men were raping Hindu women. The rallying cry for the Muzaffarnagar communal violence was 'Beti Bachao' (Save Daughters)—which here connoted 'save your daughters from Muslim men' (who, it was implied, may either rape your daughter or fall in love with and marry your daughter). In the election campaign that followed, the BJP president Amit Shah made speeches in western UP justifying the violence in the name of women's safety.

In an election meeting at Bijnor, addressing Dalits, Shah asked why Mayawati had given nineteen tickets to a community 'that violates the honour of sisters and daughters (*jo behen-betiyon . . . ki aabru pe haath dalta hai*)', while she had only given seventeen tickets to Dalits. This was a dog-whistle indicating to his audience that Muslims were rapists, since the BSP had nineteen Muslim and seventeen Dalit candidates![20]

Addressing a Jat Sabha in the Muzaffarnagar–Shamli area, which had suffered the worst riots in 2013, Shah said: 'No one is fond of rioting. But when a community violates the honour of our daughters and sisters, and the administration does nothing, people are forced to riot.'[21]

In reality, Muslim women were raped during the communal violence in Muzaffarnagar. The rape cases filed by women are yet to come to trial in the past six years, even as ministers in Modi's cabinet like Sanjeev Balyan visited and supported those accused of riots and rapes during the 2013 violence.[22]

It is interesting that the other common pretext for communal lynching—protecting '*gaumata*', the 'mother' cow—is also a gendered one. The Sangh outfits call upon Hindu men to assert Hindu masculinity and kill Muslim men to 'protect daughters and sisters', and to 'protect "mother" cows'. The Cobrapost sting operation Juliet recorded Sanjay Agarwal, who contested municipal elections on a BJP ticket in Muzaffarnagar in 2014, saying that he stoked fear about the safety of daughters and cows from Muslims, in order to garner votes for Modi in the election.[23]

The fact is, as the Cobrapost sting exposed, the campaign against 'love jihad', far from protecting Hindu women from violence, actually exposes them to intense politically organized and legitimized violence.

In 2018, BJP MLA from Madhya Pradesh, Gopal Parmar, offered child marriages as a solution to the 'problem' of 'love jihad'—if girls were married off in childhood, he said, Muslim men could not 'steal' them once they were adults.[24] This statement underlines, again, how this ideology does not see women as persons but as property, and how little it cares for the actual rights of women. Subjecting girls to the crime and real harm of child marriage is, in Parmar's view, okay, if it can 'protect' them from the imagined harm their community will suffer if they 'lose' them as adults to Muslim men!

Social Hierarchy Rationalized as 'Social Harmony'

Golwalkar's unabashed recommendation that Muslims either become Hindus or be made to live as second-class citizens in India, admiration for the Nazi 'race pride', etc., have become somewhat embarrassing for the RSS. They will only rarely articulate these views openly. Instead the same views are camouflaged and presented as '*samajik samrasta*' or social harmony; or the Deendayal Upadhyay concept of 'integral humanism'. These banal and benign-sounding phrases, on closer inspection, are revealed to be the same Nazi wolf in sheep's clothing.

My reader may ask, why take so much space to speak about attitudes towards minorities and oppressed castes in a book about women? If you have stayed with my book so far, the answer should be fairly clear to you. Maintaining social segregation and hierarchy, between Hindu and Muslim, between white and black, between German Aryan and Jew, all require intense control over women's sexual and reproductive rights. The South African comedian and writer Trevor Noah explains why in apartheid South Africa, he as a son of a black mother and a white father, was 'born a crime'. His birth was deemed a crime because his very existence would disprove the central tenet of the apartheid regime: that the white race was superior to the black one, and that the two could never mix.

> In any society built on institutionalized racism, race-mixing doesn't merely challenge the system as unjust, it reveals the system as unsustainable and incoherent. Race-mixing proves that races can mix—and in a lot of cases, want to mix. Because a mixed person embodies that rebuke to the logic of the system, race-mixing becomes a crime worse than treason.[25]

Likewise, if Muslim men and Hindu women fall in love with each other, the Sangh feels impelled to call it 'jihad', not 'love'—because admitting it is 'love' means admitting that

Hindus and Muslims can love each other, that women are not the property of their respective communities, and that Muslim men are not evil. To admit all this is to declare the very premise of Hindu Rashtra untenable and incoherent.

As we saw in our discussion of the Mahabharata and the Gita in the very first chapter, women's autonomy has for very long been abhorred and feared in this part of the world, for its power to disrupt the foundations of the caste system, by creating an 'intermixture of castes'. The violence against inter-caste and interfaith marriages both stem from a similar motive: the boundaries between castes and faiths and the notion of discriminating between human beings on the basis of caste and faith hierarchies are threatened every time a woman moves freely across these boundaries. Violence against minorities and oppressed communities inevitably also requires violence against women, not only from those targeted communities, but also those from the dominant community.

When Modi quoted Deendayal Upadhyay to exhort BJP activists to 'treat Muslims as your own', adding that Muslims must be 'refined/cleansed' (*parishkrit*) not 'appeased/rewarded' (*puraskrit*) or 'shunned' (*tiraskrit*), there were many approving media headlines that read it as an 'integral humanist' reproof to communal colleagues. But a close look at what Upadhyay actually wrote makes it clear that there isn't much of a gap between Upadhyay's vision of a Hindu India and Golwalkar's Nazi-inspired vision of a Hindu India.[26]

In a piece titled '*Akhand Bharat*' (Undivided India) in the RSS organ *Panchjanya* on 24 August 1953, Upadhyay wrote:

... the separatist and anti-national attitude of the Muslim community is the greatest obstruction to Akhand Bharat (Undivided India). The creation of Pakistan is the triumph of this attitude. Those who have doubts about Akhand Bharat feel that the Muslim will not change his policy. If this is so, then the continuance of six crore Muslims in India would be highly detrimental to the interest of India. Would any Congressman say that Muslims should be driven out of India? If not, then they will have to be assimilated into the national life of this country. If this assimilation is possible [of Muslims] within geographically divided India, then it won't take long for the rest of the geographical territory to assimilate with India. But apart from making Muslims Indian, we must also change the 30-year old policy of Hindu Muslim unity, which Congress adopted on a wrong basis . . . If we want unity, we must display Indian nationalism which is Hindu nationalism, and Indian culture which is Hindu culture. We must adopt it as our guiding principle.[27]

So, where Golwalkar said that Muslims must 'adopt the Hindu culture' and 'lose their separate existence to merge in the Hindu race', Upadhyay too is saying that no Hindu–Muslim unity is possible or desirable as long as Muslims have a separate, distinct religious and cultural identity. For 'unity', Upadhyay says, Muslims must accept 'Indian nationalism which is Hindu nationalism, and Indian culture which is Hindu culture', or else be 'driven out of India'. When Modi encourages RSS and BJP colleagues to follow Upadhyay and 'refine Muslims and treat them as your own', those RSS and BJP colleagues, who have read Upadhyay's own writings, are likely to interpret that to mean, 'treat Muslims as Hindus, teach them to be Hindus'.

Similarly, Modi in an interview to the TV channel Network18[28] as well as in his Independence Day speech in 2016 spoke of 'social harmony' (samajik samrasta), a phrase that the RSS uses to describe their view of ideal, harmonious (and hierarchical) social relations in a Hindu nation. What will be the position of women, Dalits and religious minorities in this 'harmonious' hierarchy?

A selection of Modi's speeches have been compiled in a book *Samajik Samrasta*.[29] In it, Modi preaches '*Samar nahin, samrasta*'—that is, 'not war but harmony'. He claims that B.R. Ambedkar sought *not to* wage war on caste and make a break with the Hindu religion and Hindutva politics, but to 'unite' Hindu society. This, of course, contradicts the central tenet of Ambedkar's political philosophy, which called for the 'annihilation of caste',[30] not the 'rationalization of caste' or the 'unification of Hindus'. Modi's definition of 'social harmony' in the speeches compiled in the book, specifically excludes Muslims and Christians. One of the speeches in the book has a long passage against the slogan 'Dalit Muslim Bhai-Bhai' (Dalits and Muslims are brothers)—instead, throughout his book, he refers to Muslims only as 'foreign invaders', and alludes to the 'cruelty of Muslims'.

Modi claims in his book that Ambedkar, addressing 20,000 Dalit women at the 'Convention of Federation of Scheduled Caste' in 1942, exhorted, 'You are the Lakshmi of the house. You have to be cautious that nothing unfortunate befalls the household.' Did Ambedkar really say this? On 20 July 1942, Ambedkar did address the All India Depressed Classes Women's Conference, which was attended by 20,000–25,000 women. He urged women not to be in a hurry to marry early, and to adopt family planning. Most importantly, he said, 'Let each girl who marries stand up to her husband, claim to be her husband's friend and equal, and refuse to be his slave.'[31] Elsewhere, Ambedkar excoriated the Hindu Brahminical order that makes women gateways to the castes and polices those gateways rigidly. He pushed for women's freedom in the form of the Hindu Code Bill in the teeth of orthodox opposition. The 'Ambedkar' in Modi's speech does none of these things. Instead, Modi remoulds Ambedkar in Manu's or the RSS's image, to suit the 'social harmony' philosophy. In a travesty of the real Ambedkar, Modi's 'Ambedkar' merely repeats corny lines about women as *'ghar ki Lakshmi'* that could have been taken from countless conservative Hindi films. So, the concept of 'social harmony' disguises inequalities as 'harmony', using soothing phrases assuring the oppressed of their divinity. In this framework, women or Dalits who struggle for equality and dignity are accused of disrupting social harmony and introducing discord. If inequality and oppression are harmonious, struggles against inequality and oppression are, of course, disruptive and discordant!

Nothing reveals the true import of the 'social harmony' of the RSS and BJP more than their attitude towards the Ranveer Sena. In the 1990s, the Ranveer Sena—a feudal private militia backed by a galaxy of top leaders from the

BJP and the JDU, which shared close ideological affinities with the RSS—conducted a series of massacres of Dalit landless poor in Bihar, to deter them from asserting their social, economic and electoral dignity and autonomy. The assertion of Dalit women for dignity, against the feudal sense of sexual entitlement over their bodies and lives, was an important aspect of class struggles in Bihar at the time. Agricultural labourers, both men and women, overwhelmingly from the Dalit and extremely backward oppressed castes, waged struggles for the right to organize, the right to negotiate for wages, the right to claim legally mandated entitlement to ceiling-surplus land[32] and commons land, and the right to vote. These struggles were met with an organized political reaction. In 1996, the Ranveer Sena conducted its first massacre—slaughtering twenty-one people in the Bathani Tola hamlet, most of whom with one exception were women and children from Dalit and extremely backward Muslim communities. A series of massacres followed, the worst of which was the Laxmanpur Bathe massacre in which fifty-eight men, women and children were killed in their sleep. The Cobrapost sting caught many Ranveer Sena men on video boasting of having committed the massacres and receiving funding and arms from senior BJP leaders.[33]

Bihar's BJP leader and cabinet minister in Modi's first and second terms, Giriraj Singh, once described the Ranveer Sena chief Brahmeshwar Singh as 'a Gandhian thinker and a farmer leader, who had faith in peace and social harmony'.[34] Brahmeshwar Singh himself had said in his last interview before his death, to Dan Morrison of

New York Times, 'Violence for the restoration of peace and harmony is not a sin.'[35] So, some of the worst massacres of Dalit landless poor women and children in India are described by the BJP and by the Ranveer Sena as actions to restore 'peace and social harmony'. Why did Brahmeshwar Singh use the word 'restoration'? Because it is the Dalit men and women *victims* who are accused of *disrupting* the harmonious hierarchies by demanding equality and refusing subservience and subjugation.

'Family' and 'Home' as Nucleus of 'Social Harmony'

One of the central metaphors of the Sangh's 'social harmony' is that of the 'home' or 'ghar', and its sister-term 'family' or 'parivar'. This metaphor is invoked to valorize the patriarchal family and subjugation of women inside families. RSS and BJP leader Ram Madhav, in an op-ed article on India's Independence Day 2017, claimed that the 'genius of India' is 'rooted in its religio-social institutions like state, family, caste, guru and festival'.[36] Note: Madhav counts caste—which Ambedkar had branded as 'anti-national' and which he had sought to annihilate— as part of the corpus comprising 'the genius of India'. Madhav's piece celebrates social hierarchies as 'Indian' and derides constitutional values and what Ambedkar called 'constitutional morality' as alien 'Western liberal discourse'. And those social hierarchies include not only caste but also 'family', because for the Sangh, gender hierarchies within the patriarchal 'family' are valorized rather than seen as something requiring change.

Journalist Neha Dixit, writing about a visit to a camp of the RSS women's wing Rashtra Sevika Samiti, notes that Rashtriya Swayamsevak Sangh means 'National Volunteer Corps', while in contrast 'the term Rashtra Sevika denotes women who serve the nation. This difference in the meaning does hint at the conventional humble service that is expected of a self-sacrificing woman. The sense of autonomy and self-choice that are associated with the word "volunteer" are notably missing.'[37]

Dixit writes that the Rashtra Sevika cadres 'are categorically told that the difference between the Rashtra Sevika Samiti and other women's organizations is that unlike others they do not fight for women's rights, instead they fight to create a Hindu rashtra'.[38] A Rashtra Sevika Samiti leader explained to Dixit, 'We are not feminists, we are family-ists.'[39] In these camps, young Hindu women are indoctrinated to believe that they need arms training to kill Muslims who are lustful invaders and rapists. The 'love jihad' bogey is propagated among the young women, with one leader saying, 'Muslim boys are encouraged to elope with our girls. The money they are paid to elope and marry a Hindu girl depends on the caste of the girl.'[40]

The idea of 'family' that the Samiti propagates is a strictly hierarchical one in which women must be subordinate to the wishes and decisions of their husbands and autonomy is discouraged and frowned upon. The Samiti manual says, '. . . after marriage, a girl will have many responsibilities in her new home. It is not advisable for her to bring disquiet by refusing to compromise. If ordained by her fate, her husband will permit her to study.'[41]

As long as women remain submissive and obedient, harmony within the family remains intact. Even domestic violence must be borne quietly, stifling one's screams, to prioritize maintaining family harmony. Dixit asked Sharda, one of the Samiti leaders, 'What advice would you give to a victim of wife-beating?' The reply justified wife-beating: 'Don't parents admonish their children for misbehaviour? Just as a child must adjust to his/her parents, so must a wife act keeping in mind her husband's mood and must avoid irritating him. Only this can keep the family together.'[42] Sharda's reply is not an aberration; this is the standard Sangh understanding on domestic violence. In an interview published in 1995, VHP women's wing leader Krishna Sharma defended wife-beating in almost identical words: 'Don't parents admonish their children for misbehaviour? . . . a wife must act keeping in mind her husband's moods and must avoid irritating him . . . if she learns to stifle her screams, the matter will remain within the four walls of the house. Otherwise every house will become a "Mahabharata".'[43]

Feminist assertions of women's autonomy are painted by Sangh ideology as Western-inspired disruptions of the harmonious Indian family. Oppressive social practices are all rationalized as having evolved to 'protect' women from rapacious Muslims.

Constitution vs *Manusmriti*

Ram Madhav's article suggested that the Modi government was the first government in independent India that was true to the values that define the 'genius of India', which is why 'the mob is enjoying it'.[44] His use of the word 'mob' is a deliberate jibe at the protests against lynch-mob violence; he is implying that those distressed and anguished at lynch-mob violence are Westernized elites, who are cut off from the 'genius of India'.

Is it true that only the worst, the most dehumanizing social hierarchies and practices of India represent India's 'genius' while any attempt to resist these practices— whether these are caste atrocities, communal lynchings, 'honour killings', sati, or dowry/domestic violence—is alien and foreign? It is worth recalling Ambedkar's words here:

> Constitutional morality is not a natural sentiment . . .
> We must realize that our people have yet to learn it.
> Democracy in India is only a top dressing on an Indian
> soil which is essentially undemocratic.[45]

Here, Ambedkar acknowledges that 'Indian soil' might be 'naturally' undemocratic—but instead of celebrating this undemocratic Indian soil as the 'genius of India', he advocated that the soil be supplied with democratic nutrients to nurture constitutional morality. In his speech in the Constituent Assembly on the adoption of the Constitution, on 25 November 1949, Ambedkar made it very clear *why* independence and liberty were precious in his analysis:

> What are we having this liberty for? We are having this
> liberty in order to reform our social system, which is full
> of inequality, discrimination and other things, which
> conflict with our fundamental rights.[46]

If for Ambedkar, 'liberty' from the British colonial rule was the freedom to take responsibility for our own society and strive for change and reform, 'liberty' for the Sangh is the liberty to *resist* change, and deride any striving for social change and reform as 'inspired by the West'. Inequality and discrimination are celebrated by the Sangh as 'India's native genius', and those seeking to change and challenge them are 'anti-national'.

People's movements in India—the movements of women, Dalits, workers, peasants, the left, socialists, environmentalists, civil libertarians—all represent the striving of Indians to be the best version of themselves. These movements have routinely been branded as 'alien' and 'Westernized' by fascists, while fascists the world over have always claimed to be 'organic' sons of the soil. The truth is, though, that Indian fascists are, as we have seen, inspired by Hitler and Nazism which was 'foreign' to India. They appeal to Indians to be the worst version of themselves, drawing on the most illiberal tendencies and most oppressive traditions.

The Constitution, drafted in large part by Ambedkar, was an attempt to appeal to the best in Indians, calling upon 'we the people' to protect the rights of all citizens and people, especially the oppressed sections and minorities.

Ambedkar had mobilized people to burn the *Manusmriti*, as the fountainhead of obnoxious anti-Dalit and anti-women rules that continue to govern society. In contrast, the RSS wanted the Indian Constitution to be based on the *Manusmriti*.

The RSS mouthpiece, *Organiser*, in its editorial dated 30 November 1949, a few days after the ratification of the

Constitution drafted in Ambedkar's leadership, complained that the Indian Constitution was inspired by the West and did not reflect the native genius of the *Manusmriti*:

> But in our Constitution there is no mention of the unique constitutional developments in ancient Bharat. Manu's laws were written long before Lycurgus of Sparta or Solon of Persia. To this day laws as enunciated in the *Manusmriti* excite the admiration of the world and elicit spontaneous obedience and conformity. But to our constitutional pundits that means nothing.

Who was the *Organizer* referring to when it claimed that the *Manusmriti* was admired the world over? It was Ambedkar who, in his writings, had revealed the ideological link between the *Manusmriti* that had inspired the German philosopher Nietzsche, who in turn inspired Hitler. The RSS leaders were in turn inspired by Hitler and Mussolini.[47]

Even today RSS and BJP leaders continue to seek out ways in which to rehabilitate and 'normalize' the *Manusmriti*. Writing a separate hagiographic piece on RSS founder Golwalkar, Modi even described Ambedkar, the fighter against Manuvad who burnt the *Manusmriti*, as a 'modern Manu'.[48]

Nowhere is the BJP's and Sangh's Manuvadi vision more apparent than in their attitude to women and Dalits. Adityanath (Ajay Singh Bisht, who styles himself 'Yogi Adityanath') was handpicked by Modi, Amit Shah and the RSS to become the chief minister of

UP—India's largest state. In a detailed write-up titled '*Matrshakti: Bharatiya Shakti ke Sandarbh Mein*', which was uploaded in 2014 on his own website, Adityanath echoed the *Manusmriti* to write that according to Hindu scriptures, '[W]omen are not capable of being left free or independent . . . women need male protection from birth to death . . . a woman is protected in her childhood by her father, by her husband in her youth and by her son in her old age.' This idea of women being under men's protection all their lives (father, husband and son) is straight from the *Manusmriti*.

After Adityanath became the chief minister, some journalists began exposing his attitude towards women, citing the article on his website.[49] Subsequently, the write-up was quietly taken down from the website. Clicking on the link for the article,[50] you get a message saying: 'The resource you are looking for might have been removed.'

In the article, Adityanath is eloquent against women's freedom:

Whereas in our shastras, the greatness of women has been described, at the same time considering their importance and their decorum and dignity, the need to give them protection is also mentioned . . . Just like if you leave energy free and uncontrolled and unregulated, it may become useless and destructive, similarly '*shakti swaroopa stree*'—woman as the epitome of power—does not really need freedom, but a meaningful role with protection and channelization . . . For only such controlled and protected women power will give birth to and raise great men and when required step out of home to the battlefield to destroy evil powers.

Here, Adityanath echoes the sentiments expressed in the Gita and the Mahabharata (see Chapter I in this book) where women's sexual and reproductive powers are viewed as both beneficial and dangerous and potentially destructive to the caste patriarchy.

Adityanath writes that women should receive education today, but only as a safety valve to stave off the dangerous urges for freedom:

Else the thoughtless storm of women's freedom of the Western world will drive them to an even more disastrous condition and it will hamper the creation and stability of the home and family and prevent the glorious rebuilding of the nation and motherland.

He vehemently opposes the idea of 33 per cent reservations for women in Parliament and assemblies, saying it would affect women's duties as mothers, daughters and sisters:

Women do already have reservations in many areas. First, analyse and assess the impact of this in gram sabhas, panchayats and local bodies. Assess and then decide whether women who are in active politics, and public life like men, whether in this process they may not lose their importance and role as mothers, daughters and sisters.

He adds, 'If men acquire women-like qualities, they become gods but when women acquire men-like qualities, they become ['*rakshasa*'] demon-like. Serious thought must be given to these issues. What if this leads to the creation of the Frankenstein's monster?'

Adityanath is not a fringe figure. It appears that he has been given the status of potential successor to Modi. He is not only the chief minister of the politically crucial state of UP, he also seems to be the favoured star campaigner[51] for the BJP in elections all over the country. His ideas, in my opinion, provide the fodder for the BJP's real 'Mann ki Baat'. By mainstreaming Adityanath, it seems that the BJP is preparing the grounds to turn India into a Hindu nation. And if a fascist Hindu nation were ever to come into being, we should expect *Manusmriti*-inspired ideas to be enshrined as law, imprisoning India's women and endorsing and enforcing the subjugation of women and Dalits.

Islamophobia Disguised as Feminism

My reader may ask: 'You critique the *Manusmriti*, but aren't the religious texts of Islam or Christianity just as misogynist?'

Most organized religions have historically been misogynistic and have proclaimed women to be naturally inferior or subordinate to men. Any theological state is, therefore, likely to have a misogynistic constitution and laws. The example of Saudi Arabia is a handy one. I keep meeting Indian people who suggest that India needs laws like Saudi Arabia that punish rape with stoning or other 'harsh' measures. My standard reply is: Saudi Arabia has a particularly misogynistic state, with laws that place adult women under the 'guardianship' of men and conflate 'forbidden' consensual sexual relationships with rape—so how would its laws make Indian women safer or freer? Saudi laws define rape as the loss of 'honour' rather than the violation of consent. As a result, a rapist can avoid prosecution as long as he marries his victim.[52] In 2014, Morocco did away with a similar provision in its law after a sixteen-year-old rape victim committed suicide to avoid being forced to marry her rapist.[53] In Saudi Arabia, rape victims are afraid to complain, because they risk being punished for 'mingling' with men. In 2007, a teenage girl in Saudi Arabia had been blackmailed by a boyfriend into giving him her photograph. After she got married a few years later, she feared the photograph might be misused and asked the former boyfriend to return it. He said he would if she agreed to meet him and go for a drive with him. While she met him in his car to retrieve the photograph, a gang of seven men took them both captive and gang-raped them.[54] Her attackers received prison sentences ranging from ten months to five years, and 80 to 1,000 lashes. The woman and her former boyfriend, both rape victims, were sentenced to ninety lashes each for violating the Saudi law prohibiting a woman from meeting in private with a man who is not her husband or a relative. When the woman's lawyer appealed this verdict as unjust and spoke to the media about it, the court increased her punishment to 200 lashes and stripped her lawyer of his licence, while also increasing the sentences of the rapists. Eventually, in response to an international outcry, the Saudi king pardoned the woman and her former boyfriend.[55]

The thing is that in India, you, of course, have both Hindu and Muslim communalism. However, India's first prime minister, Jawaharlal Nehru, was right when he observed that while the communalism of both majority and minority communities were anti-democratic, the communalism of the majority was more dangerous because it was 'apt to be taken for nationalism' and could therefore lead to fascism.[56] This is exactly why Ambedkar too, while being sharply critical on many occasions of Muslim fundamentalists, was clear that 'if Hindu raj does become a fact, it will no doubt be the greatest calamity for this country . . . a menace to liberty, equality and fraternity. On that account it is incompatible with democracy. Hindu raj must be prevented at any cost.'[57] In Pakistan or Bangladesh, then, Muslim communalism is a far greater danger than the communalism of any minority, because it can masquerade as 'nationalism' and stake a claim to state power, crush democracy and usher in fascism. In India, the Sangh disguises Hindu communalism as 'nationalism' in a way that minority communalists cannot.

In India, it is Muslims who have challenged Muslim fundamentalism and communalism most consistently and steadfastly. Muslim women are at the forefront of the struggle to change anti-women Muslim personal laws. The Sangh, by posing as the champion and saviour of Muslim women from Muslim men, propagates the Islamophobic myth that Islam is uniquely patriarchal and evil; that Muslim men are the most oppressive and Muslim women the most oppressed. The same BJP that can claim that the hijab (head scarf) is a symbol of oppression of Muslim women can proclaim, through its government in Haryana, that 'ghoonghat' is the 'pride and honour' of Haryana![58]

In 1995, when I was a student at the Jawaharlal Nehru University, BJP leader, the late K.R. Malkani, came to our hostel mess to address a public meeting organized by the ABVP on women's rights and anti-women personal laws. I had been reading up on patriarchal laws in India and headed out to attend the meeting. Malkani spent much of his talk speaking about the plight of Muslim women like Shah Bano who were denied maintenance under Islamic personal law, and Muslim women oppressed by polygamy. He argued in favour of a Uniform Civil Code in India, to liberate Muslim women from their oppression. When the meeting was opened for questions, I raised my hand. I told Malkani that I agreed that Muslim personal laws were indeed unequal and called for change, and I asked him what he made of Hindu property and guardianship laws that, at the time, denied daughters the right to inherit ancestral property and decreed that a mother was not the natural guardian of her child. He replied, without missing a beat, 'Hindu women do not need property, they get married and their husbands' families take care of them.' The room full of women students, most of them new to JNU, erupted in outrage at his casual denial of equality to Hindu women. I also asked him: if polygamy was a wrong done to Muslim women, would he also condemn a Hindu BJP leader who had recently committed polygamy? Malkani replied, in some confusion, that the leader in question was not really a Hindu but an Adivasi, a tribal man, among whose community polygamy was considered acceptable. Malkani had found himself in a strange situation: he had had to admit that Adivasis were not Hindus, and that polygamy was prevalent not only among Muslims but among some Adivasi communities too that also had their own personal laws. His party, the BJP, did not openly demand abolition of personal laws of the Adivasi communities. He also could not explain why a Muslim man committing polygamy was considered the epitome of evil while making excuses for a BJP leader who did the same.

The BJP position on triple talaq displays the same double standards. Muslim women and women's organizations (including the organization to which I belong, AIPWA) have been agitating for the abolition of instant triple talaq for long. The Supreme Court judgment holding instant triple talaq to be unconstitutional and illegal is a landmark one. However, as we feminist activists know from years of personal experience, the problem of wives being arbitrarily abandoned by husbands, without any due process of legal divorce and maintenance, is hardly unique to Muslim women. Around 19 lakh Hindu women in India today (and 2.8 lakh Muslim women) have been arbitrarily abandoned by their husbands, and they too require justice. The very public example of Jasodaben is a case in point: Narendra Modi only publicly acknowledged her existence as his wife in an affidavit filed before the 2014 Lok Sabha polls. She has had to publicly correct claims by Modi's colleagues that he is unmarried, and assert that she is indeed his wife; while Modi himself has never publicly told them off for any such claims.[59] Now the question is not whether it is fair to expect Modi to treat Jasodaben as his wife, since they were both married as minors. The issue is: Modi cannot be exempt from the legal obligation to seek and secure a formal divorce, if he wishes to be free from the marriage. Modi after all has been able to live his life freely unencumbered by his marriage, whereas Jasodaben, being a woman in a patriarchal society, has been in a permanent limbo.

The attempt here is not to make a 'whatabout' point to say that if Modi and other Hindu men can be unjust to their wives, why can't Muslim men also do the same? Instead, the point is to recognize that patriarchy and misogyny are not unique to any religion or community— and feminists, unlike communalists, do not use injustices to women as a stick to beat the 'other' community with. Feminists are not interested in any competition between communities to claim, 'We treat women better than you do.' Instead, we know that patriarchal injustices in one's own community and family are the hardest to recognize because that patriarchy appears 'normal' and 'natural', whereas the patriarchy of the 'other' community or family, because unfamiliar, shocks us as 'abnormal'. Whichever community we happen to belong to, we need to practise rendering our 'own' homegrown patriarchies unfamiliar and organize to challenge them.

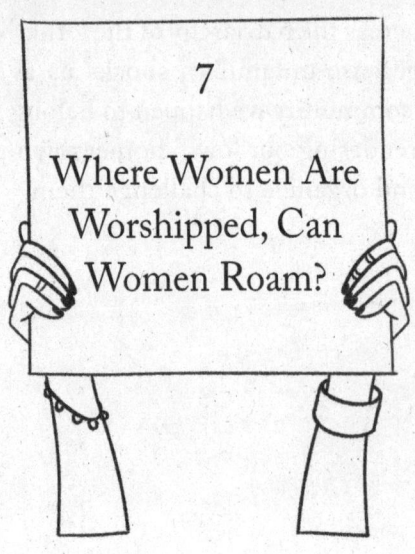

7

Where Women Are Worshipped, Can Women Roam?

Where she's worshipped, the gods roam
She's Sita, Savitri
She's Mother
She's Motherland, greater than heaven

But crashing against the walls
Her head bloody
She falls.

—Gorakh Pandey, 'Band Khidkiyon Se Takrakar'

'Yatra naryastu pujyante ramante tatra devata' or *'Jahan naari ki pooja hoti hai, vahan devata ramte hain'*—where

women are worshipped, there roam the gods. Along with 'Janani janmabhoomishcha swargaadapi gareeyasi' (Mother and Motherland are even more treasured than heaven), this is the saying that is solemnly and sententiously repeated at many an official function in India.

The question is: where women are worshipped, can women roam? *Jahan naari ki pooja hoti hai, vahan naari ram sakti hai kya?* Where the gods roam, can women roam? *Jahan devata ramte hain, vahan naari ram sakti hai kya?* Where women are worshipped, and the nation is revered as a woman, are women free and equal?

The land of one's birth (*janmabhoomi*) is often compared to the mother who birthed us (*janani*)—and this is a comforting image, suggesting that the nation nurtures us, cares for us and protects us from harm as a mother protects her children.

Let us unpack the bundle of ideas that connote 'mother' and 'motherland' in our everyday lives and our culture, to see what these ideas spell for the freedom and autonomy of women.

Mothers beyond Mothering

In the 1985 film *Parama*, Rakhi plays a 'typical' wife and mother in a Bengali household, whose life suddenly experiences an upheaval when she falls in love with an itinerant photographer. While everyone in her family refers to her as ma), the young photographer is the first in many years to call her by her name. That recognition of her individuality is what draws her to him and upends her orderly life.

When I think of 'mother', the image that leaps to my mind, naturally, is of my own mother. My mother loves her two daughters—my sister and I—fiercely. I have seen her mother, protect and nurture any number of strays (dogs, cats, squirrels, cows, buffaloes, birds and snakes), as well as trees and children.

As a ten-year-old lying on the upper berth of a train, I had an early experience of sexual harassment and abuse: a man sleeping on the adjacent berth reached around the barrier and kept touching my fingers and arms. I climbed down quietly and told my mother. She (always, even today, a nimble scaler of trees and walls) climbed up to the berth without using the ladder, so that the man would not be able to see that she had replaced me. Then she lay in wait, with her tweezers in her hand. When the man's hand came snaking around, she pinched the flesh hard with the tweezers. He yelped in pain and wrenched his hand back in a hurry. His friend and he tried to come over and accuse my mother of hurting his hand—my mother asked him what his hand had been doing on our berth anyway.

Like a mother cat or dog, she could be rather fierce when she had to protect her kids from harm, but she would also play rough-and-tumble games with us. Like many mother cats and dogs I have known who periodically smack their kids smartly over the head and demand to be left alone, she would frequently express her wish to be utterly free of mothering and household burdens. Her wish to 'escape (from us all, naturally) to the Himalayas' and just be a free spirit was something we grew up hearing about quite a lot. It is no surprise that my mother derives endless amusement from Twitter trolls—including actor Alok Nath—who refer to me as a 'bitch' or attribute canine parentage to me. 'Don't they realize we think this is a compliment?' she is fond of asking.

From her, we learned to take up causes that seemed lost and certainly unpopular: standing fearlessly and all alone on streets defending a stray dog from hostile neighbours or protecting a community park from being turned into a *vyayam shala* or *shakha* (exercise and training ground) by the local BJP Yuva Morcha. As children, we knew that she loved us dearly and was our best friend—but that she also formed equally close and loving attachments and friendships with other people closer to our age than hers.

All her life, my mother has done an inordinate amount of hands-on care-work: giving up her job to stay with and care for her ailing father, for her mother-in-law in her last years, for my father a full ten years after he had a stroke and developed Parkinson's, and for her mother in her final days.

But we would find it impossible to see her as a nurturer alone or as our sole nurturer. My dad was happiest feeding, cleaning and caring for his babies—a lot happier, I think, than he would have been as the stern, remote, authority figure, fathers are often expected to be. He taught himself to cook and cleaning the house remained his job for as long as he was able. Once, a colleague of my mother's—a handsome young man—dropped in at our place and laughed out loud to see my dad chopping vegetables and cooking. I remember feeling bemused at why he found this funny—and angry when it dawned on me that he found it absurd and unmanly for a man to be doing what he saw as 'women's work'. But my dad did not seem in the least bothered by the man's amusement. As a teenager, when I would ask him if I should not begin learning to cook, he would say, 'Oh! Once you start living on your own, your stomach and tongue will teach you to cook!'

That my mother's life, love and aspirations were not confined to us—her husband and children—was something we grew up taking for granted. Working and earning were important to her, and so my sister and I were both latch-key kids from an early age. Watching cricket matches, learning music and new languages, enjoying the privacy to read a book or take a walk undisturbed—these were all things she loved to do. She didn't let us labour under any illusion that every waking moment of hers was meant to be in service to our wants.

And then, of course, the relation between her and me was as stormy as it was warm. She and I had huge battles in my teenage years, over what, we can no longer recall.

The fights, the companionship, the games of hop-scotch and Scrabble, the sisterhood and comradeship between mother and daughter, and our openness to getting to know and appreciate or at least accept each other's (likely and unlikely) friends and each other's autonomy—this has been the salt and spice of our relationship. And that's why I am frustrated by the blandness of the mother figures I find in most mainstream Indian films and literature. How many Indian works of literature can you think of in which there is a 'mother' character who has a rich emotional life beyond mothering? There are not many—you can come up with some, but you'll have to work hard to think of them.

I remember the thrill of recognition I felt on reading these words describing Ammu in *The God of Small Things*: 'Ammu had not had the kind of education, nor read the sorts of books, nor met the sorts of people, that might have influenced her to think the way she did. She was just that sort of animal.'[1] My mother too is 'that sort of animal'—a feminist by instinct rather than by training.

That novel could bring alive an Ammu who was a loving mother while also being a complete and contradictory human being, capable of being overly stern with her children, and capable also of 'breaking the "Love Laws"—the laws that lay down who should be loved and how. And how much'.[2]

It is notable that Comrade E.M.S. Namboodiripad, in his polemical attack on Roy and her novel, wrote, that 'the author has accused her own mother of indulging in deviant sexuality. Yet Mary Roy takes pride in the "beautiful work" by her daughter. Why is it so?' In answer to his own question, Comrade E.M.S. wrote that this was because in the novelist's vision, 'sexual anarchy' was not a moral failing but the mark of a 'revolutionary spirit'. He wrote that he was fine with being portrayed unfavourably by Roy in this novel, because he was proud of being a communist, a real revolutionary rather than someone whom Roy considered revolutionary for displaying 'deviant sexuality'.[3] This passage tells us a lot about how, even for some on the left, the notion of a mother who divorces the father of her children and falls in love—and moreover makes love—across caste boundaries with a Dalit man is scandalous and morally repugnant. Once a mother, a woman must be nothing *but* a mother, it is implied: any desires of her own (especially those that break caste laws) are taboo. As a communist myself, I can say that if you can't celebrate and work for the breaking of the Brahminical patriarchal 'Love Laws', you can't really be a revolutionary in India!

Pedestal or Prison?

Gorakh Pandey's poem, with which this chapter begins, starkly underlines the contrast between our society's worship of woman as Mother and Motherland, and the fact that women in the same society are violently confined by locked windows in their homes. As an anonymous African American feminist said, 'A pedestal is as much a prison as any other small, confined space.'

By 'worshipping' women as mothers or as goddesses, we disguise that we are denying them recognition as equal human beings. Divinity erases their humanity, confining them to the roles and ideals for which they are 'worshipped'. Satyajit Ray's haunting and disturbing film *Devi* is the story of a girl for whom the pedestal of worship becomes a nightmare. She loses her mind when she is overnight drawn up from the role of a flesh-and-blood woman, wife and daughter-in-law to being worshipped as a mother goddess.

Tanika Sarkar, writing about gender ideology in Bengal, observed, 'Motherhood and nurture are, indeed, figures and ideals worth celebrating. The problem lies partly with the gendering of nurture and the collapsing of womanhood entirely and exclusively within this single frame.'[4] Surely we can love our mothers—and appreciate motherhood and nurture—without insisting that nurture is women's work *alone*, and equating womanhood with *nothing but* motherhood and nurture?

Indian cinema and literature revere the 'mother' as a figure of sacrifice, suffering without complaint, and as a source of moral affirmation. '*Mere paas Ma hai*' or 'I have Mother' is the iconic retort of Shashi Kapoor in *Deewar* to his brother's boasts about his ill-gotten 'buildings, property, bank balance, car and bungalow'. The same popular culture that reveres the mother-figure, however, caricatures the modern young woman who demands equality or freedom as being responsible for breaking up homes and mistreating old parents-in-law. Tanika Sarkar writes, 'The woman to be protected, respected, adored is then the mother-woman. The more she is adored, the more socially sanctioned and legitimized is the hostility and the distrust against the non-mother.'[5]

Did Our Foremothers Never Yearn for Freedom?

Over and over, in popular culture, we are told that the mother-figure, silent and self-sacrificing, performing her labours of love for her family without complaint is the 'authentic' Indian woman, and the woman who demands equality and chafes at confinement to domestic roles is infected by 'Western' values. In 1994, as a JNU student, a friend and I had given a short talk on gender and feminism at a workshop hosted by my student organization. After our talk, a young man— a first-year MA student who was a new entrant to JNU—

asked me (and other young women in the room): 'My grandmother was satisfied and happy being a wife and mother, why, then are you women dissatisfied and unhappy?'

Is it really true that our grandmothers were 'happy' being confined to domestic roles and did not yearn for freedom? That figure of the silent, self-sacrificing woman who loves her endless household labours is a myth. The yearning for freedom is no modern, foreign import: it is a human urge that women have shared across the world. Here is Sumangalamata, a Buddhist nun writing in 600 BC, celebrating her freedom from 'kitchen drudgery' and her 'unscrupulous' husband:

> A woman well set free! How free I am,
> How wonderfully free, from kitchen drudgery.
> Free from the harsh grip of hunger,
> And from empty cooking pots,
> Free too of that unscrupulous man,
> The weaver of sunshades.

> (Translated by historians Uma Chakravarti and Kum Kum Roy.)[6]

Another Buddhist nun, Mutta, writing in the same period, rejoiced, 'So free am I/ So gloriously free/ Free from three petty things—From mortar, from pestle and from my twisted lord . . .' (Translated by historians Uma Chakravarti and Kum Kum Roy).[7]

Our grandmothers, we are told, were perfectly content and happy performing the duties of wife and mother, feeding and nurturing their families, being the icon—in every home—of the bountiful motherland, and seeing the *mangalsutra*/thali/sindur as a woman's ultimate goal. Did they never desire to be free from this image and its burdens?

During the nationalist movement, many prominent nationalists too told us that even if colonial power ruled India, Indian mothers remained safe repositories of an essentially unsullied Indianness. For many nationalists, freedom for such mothers meant the *freedom to be happy and content in the role of wives and mothers, without colonial meddling*—not the freedom to go to school or demand equality with men. Even if India were not free, such nationalists argued, the sanctity of the Indian family and home must at least remain free from any colonial interference—and for this, it was important that Indian women remained 'free' from any desires or experiences that might make them dissatisfied with their lives.

A Caged Bird

Rashsundari Debi, a devout nineteenth-century Bengali woman who secretly taught herself to write from a devotional book, wrote the first autobiography in the Bengali language. A child bride and a wife and mother in a conservative upper-caste landlord family that disapproved of education for girls and women, did she see the tasks of nurturing assigned to her as emotionally fulfilling?

We began this book with a discussion of the prison walls of patriarchy. Rashsundari repeatedly used the metaphor of prison to describe her own life as a daughter-in-law, wife and mother.

She wrote about her identity in her marital home: 'The name that I had brought from my father's home has been lost. Here I am just the mother.'[8] The generic, abstract role of 'mother' swallowed up her individual identity and even her name.

On being sent to her in-laws' house as a child bride, she spoke bitterly of being 'caged for life', 'given a life sentence', but said that 'since I had to spend my life with these people, I eventually became a tamed bird'.[9]

The contrast between that abstract role of 'ma' and the painfully loving bond between mother and child is most striking when Rashsundari writes of her anguish at lacking the freedom, as a mere daughter, to go and be with her own mother at the latter's deathbed. That passage in her autobiography reminds us that even if her marital home was free of any violence, it was no less a prison and she was no less a slave, with her humanity being subservient to the household duties assigned to her.

Writing of her mother, she said, 'She always missed me bitterly, she tried hard to get me to visit her. But I have been locked up in a prison ever since I came here. I could never be allowed to visit her because household chores here would suffer. If ever I had to go to her on some ceremonial occasion, I was like a prisoner let out on parole, I had to be back within a couple of days. At least ten to fifteen people, two guards, two maidservants accompanied me on the boat-ride.'[10]

Rashsundari's lifelong sorrow was that she was not allowed to visit her dying mother one last time. She rails at God, asking why he created her a woman:

Why was I born a woman? Shame on my life! Who in all this world is as loving as the mother? It is hardly an exaggeration to call her the representative of the Great Lord. I did have this priceless treasure in my mother, but I could not look after her. Is there anything in the world to match this sorrow? Had I been her son, I would fly like a bird to reach her side when I got news of her end. What was I to do, I was behind bars, I was shut up in a cage.[11]

Single-handedly cooking two meals a day for twenty-five people and caring for her blind mother-in-law, Rashsundari compared herself to a blind, dumb beast of burden: 'I spoke to no one, I could hardly see anyone beyond my veil. My eyes were covered, like the eyes of the oil-presser's bullock. . . . This was how young married women were supposed to work.'[12] This is a very far cry from the language of the nationalists who romanticized the mother-figure as the very epitome of joy and contentment for women.

Forbidden Desires

For Rashsundari, education was very much an affair of the heart, a forbidden desire, a 'yearning', thwarted—as was Radha's desire for Krishna—by vigilant in-laws and endless chores. She wrote of people's claims that education for women 'leads to disaster, women should not even touch pen and paper'. And yet, she observed: 'But my heart would not accept this, it was forever yearning.'[13]

Tanika Sarkar observes, 'It is interesting that orthodox critics of women's education were convinced of an equation between the woman's intellectual desires and her sexual immorality . . . If a woman was educated, she must be immoral.'[14]

Even today, in the twenty-first century, we have a politics that cannot speak about adult women students without painting them as sexually 'immoral', and fantasizing about their sex lives in images that disguise titillation with shock and disgust! BJP MLA Gyan Dev Ahuja said '3000 used condoms'[15] were found every day on the JNU campus; BJP MP Subramanian Swamy likes to say that 'modern girls' and feminist and left activists, especially those educated in universities, are ' Naxalites' who have 'free sex';[16] a 'dossier' prepared by a JNU faculty member and BJP supporter Hari Ram Mishra described the university as a 'den of organized sex racket'.[17]

Patriarchy codes all desires of women—sexual, intellectual and (feminist/revolutionary) political—as dangerous. No surprise, since these desires are indeed dangerous for patriarchy!

Blessed Kaliyug

As we have seen in the very first chapter of this book, the spectre of the autonomous woman who marries of her own choice, talks back to her husband and in-laws, dictates terms to them and is sexually promiscuous is seen as the very embodiment of the horror of the degenerate Kaliyug, posing a dire threat to the whole social order.

But for Rashsundari, Kaliyug is welcome, because now girls are allowed education:

> Blessed, blessed be this Kaliyug . . . it is deplorable that I was not allowed to educate myself because I was a woman. How very lucky are girls of this generation! These days many try to educate their daughters. Whatever others may say, I think this is a most positive development.[18]

Rashsundari, then, was no 'content' foremother of ours, saying '*ghor* Kaliyug *aa gaya*' (the terrible Kaliyug has arrived) about modern girls craving freedom—she was a woman who craved freedom herself, and rejoiced at Kaliyug because of the possibility that girls and women could finally be free and spared a caged and confined existence that she had endured, in which she had had to learn in secrecy.

Rashsundari's enthusiasm for a Kaliyug that could not open the doors of learning to women is in sharp contrast to some prominent nationalists of her time who saw the spectre of a disastrous Kaliyug in the attempts to educate women and persons of oppressed castes. If Rashsundari loved reading and writing, so did another nineteenth-century child bride, Rakhmabai of Maharashtra, whose story offers us a way to see how education for women and

oppressed castes was virulently opposed as a threat to the
social order—i.e., the caste-patriarchal hierarchy—by some
of the stalwarts of India's freedom struggle.

A Woman Dazzled by the Flame of Learning

Unlike Rashsundari, Rakhmabai was from the Sutar
(carpenter) community, not part of the most rigid and
restrictive Brahmin caste. Her mother was a widow who
had remarried, and her stepfather (a doctor and reformist)
refused to send Rakhmabai to live with her husband when
she reached puberty. Instead, he insisted that Rakhmabai
be kept at their home till she was older, and till her husband
bettered himself by getting an education. As Rakhmabai
grew up, she received an education and, through her
parents, was exposed to various social reformers.

At the age of twelve, and supported by her parents,
Rakhmabai rejected the marriage that she had been bound
to as a child and refused to join her husband. She pointed
out that while she was educated, her husband had wasted all
efforts to educate himself. She declared that she would like
to continue her education, not be shackled to a marriage
to which she had not consented. At the age of fifteen, she
wrote open letters (anonymously published in the *Times of
India*) arguing against child marriage and expressing her
deep desire to continue her education.

Rakhmabai became the centre of a stormy legal battle
between 1884 and 1888. While reformers saw her case
as a chance to demand a raising of the age of consent,
orthodox nationalists were outraged and enraged at her

sheer audacity. Rakhmabai's husband went to court in 1884, demanding the 'restitution of his conjugal rights'. In 1885, a British judge, Justice R.H. Pinhey, pointed out that 'restitution of conjugal rights' was a provision of English law meant for consenting adults, that would not apply to a marriage under traditional Hindu law. He also added that Rakhmabai had been wed as a child and refused to compel her to cohabitate with her husband.

In 1886, following loud and sustained opposition to the Pinhey verdict, there was a retrial. In 1887, another British judge, Justice Farran, ordered Rakhmabai (who was now sixteen) to 'go live with her husband or face six months of imprisonment'. Rakhmabai said she preferred prison to a forced marriage. Eventually, her marriage was dissolved by Queen Victoria, and her husband agreed to a settlement, giving up his claim over Rakhmabai in exchange for Rs 2000. Rakhmabai's struggle paved the way for raising of the age of consent from ten to twelve years in colonial India.

In March 1887, even as the debate raged on, none other than Bal Gangadhar Tilak, the towering nationalist figure, brought his censure to weigh in against Rakhmabai. Tilak is famous for his declaration: 'Swaraj [self-rule] is my birthright and I will have it at all costs.' But on the basis of what he said about Rakhmabai, it would seem that Tilak did not want women to have swaraj over their own lives. Swaraj for Hindu women, it seemed, would in Tilak's eyes amount to Hindu men losing swaraj inside their own homes! To Tilak and his supporters, women who demanded swaraj for themselves were evidence of the dangers of giving women a 'Western' education. He wrote:

We agree that the upliftment of our women is necessary. We would, however, like to say to these reformers that this will never be achieved by women like Rakhmabai who is strutting around claiming a tiny piece of turmeric root has turned her yellow [i.e., who is putting on airs on achieving a tiny taste of education]. Today thousands of men are living happily with their underage wives. When that's the case, is it not a bit much when a woman dazzled by the flame of learning demands in court that she be granted a divorce now that her husband is no longer good enough for her?[19]

Tilak's utter contempt for Rakhmabai's intellectual aspirations and achievements can be felt in the sting of his words—and his utter disbelief that a woman could dare to challenge her subordination to her husband.

Caste, Patriarchy and the Spectre of Kaliyug

Tilak had opposed education for the oppressed castes and for women, on the grounds that it would strip them of the training they needed to do the tasks allotted to them by Brahminical patriarchy, and that it would in fact upend caste and gender hierarchies. The spectre of Kaliyug where the (Brahminical patriarchal) world would turn upside down is very apparent in his writings.

Tilak wanted a full education to be restricted to those who had a 'natural inclination' for it—and he assumed that the non-Brahmin castes, especially the backward castes and Dalits, had no inclination for education. The latter should only be given 'the education befitting their rank and station in life'.[20] He was quite explicit about his anxieties: 'English education encouraged the people to deny caste restrictions and the spread of English education among the natives will bring down the caste system.'[21] He held that reformers like Jyotiba Phule sought, through education, 'to dispel through the land any reverence that might be felt for the Brahmins'.[22]

Tilak made it clear that any education that might encourage a farmer's, blacksmith's or cobbler's child or a sex-worker's child to become a scholar instead would threaten the social rankings and occupations assigned by the Brahminical order. Likewise, he strongly opposed any education that might encourage girls to see scholarship as their goal, rather than the duties of a wife and mother.

He wrote, 'A girl preparing her lessons till 10 a.m. and remaining at school till 5 p.m. will become a regular boy student and is quite likely to forget that there are other duties incumbent on her,' and as a result, education might 'make them [girls] feel a sense of superiority over their partners'.[23]

In Tilak's worldview, we can easily recognize the ideology of caste- and gender-appropriate 'innate/natural qualities and duties' and caste-and-gender hierarchies that we have already encountered in the Mahabharata and the Gita. If a child born in the cobbler caste is assumed to be 'naturally' fit to be a cobbler and unfit for education, likewise a girl is assumed to be 'naturally' suited for the roles of a wife and mother and unfit for education. Educating 'lower' castes and women threatened the Brahminical order, which was claimed to be a 'natural' one.

Tilak obstinately insisted that 'the object of female education is not to make the woman the equal of man . . . it must also be remembered that women having to perform the wifely and maternal duties require a fund of energy to perform them satisfactorily'.[24] Energy required for 'wifely and maternal duties' must not be dissipated in learning.

Just to put things in perspective, let us remind ourselves that Rashsundari began stealing time from her unending 'wifely and maternal' duties to teach herself to read in 1834. Her autobiography was published first in 1868, and then an expanded version was published in 1888. Rashsundari—a child bride who had not been given an 'English education' or any education—felt no attachment or sense of achievement over her 'wifely and maternal duties' and instead yearned to read and write. What seemed an approaching disaster to Tilak was welcomed by Rashsundari as the 'blessed Kaliyug' where the doors of education could finally let in those hitherto excluded.

Why, you may ask, am I spending so much time recounting history? Isn't the past over and done with? Women no longer have to face what Rashsundari or Rakhmabai had to, right?

Well, flip back to the previous chapter, to the essay by Yogi Adityanath who was handpicked by the BJP to be the chief minister of UP, where he demanded that posts in Parliament and Assemblies be reserved for women only after an assessment to see if 'women who are in active politics and public life like men' might not be losing their 'role as mothers, daughters and sisters'. The same essay also argued for women to be kept under the strict control of men so that their '*matrshakti*' (maternal energy) might not be dissipated. The politics of the Sangh Parivar is pushing hard to wind the clock back a couple of centuries—forcing women and oppressed castes in India to respond to debates which many had considered long settled.

Imagining the nation as a mother and a mother goddess, valorizing and worshipping women as divine goddesses, is fully compatible with treating women as less than human. In fact, the very ideology of 'worship' for mother and motherland seems designed to disguise and rationalize the restrictions on the autonomy of women. The real live woman yearns to breathe free—but her desire for freedom is castigated and delegitimized as a betrayal of her role as mother and miniature icon of the motherland. The unique, specific personalities and experiences of each of our own mothers are undermined and rendered invisible in our culture—what remains visible is only bland, abstract, generic 'mothers', each of whom could easily be substituted by another. Womanhood and motherhood, as well as motherland are all worshipped in India—but women and mothers in India are not free.

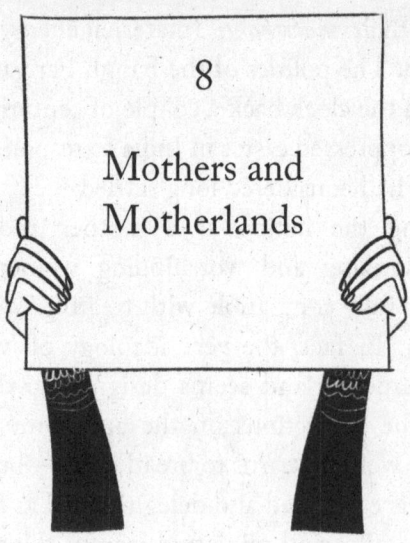

8

Mothers and
Motherlands

Just as 'daughters in danger' is an ideological pretext for violence against Dalits and minorities, 'Mothers/Motherland in danger' is also a pretext for terrible violence against minorities and oppressed nationalities.

The idea of 'mother' connotes love and acceptance. And yet, the idea of a 'Motherland' is so often used to rationalize horrific acts of violence and coercion.

In the conflict areas where we are told 'the Motherland is being defended', what consequences does the presence of armed forces in civilian areas have for the autonomy of girls and women?

Whose Mother?

Who does the mother nation need to be defended from? If the nation is imagined as the mother's body, any dispute over its borders is pictured as an act of aggression against the body and the honour of the mother nation. Political disputes are instead treated as primordial emotional matters—disguising the fact that nations routinely hold hard-headed negotiations and diplomatic bargains with each other. A good son (it's usually a son) of the mother nation can always, only, be a soldier, violent towards some external or internal enemy.

Most disturbing of all is the image of the mother nation being weaponized against the nation's own citizens, especially its religious minorities. Equating Mother India with a Hindu mother goddess, the Sangh Parivar insists that Muslims prove their patriotism and sense of national belonging by chanting 'Bharat Mata Ki Jai' (Victory to Mother India) and singing 'Vande Mataram'—the song that was the rallying cry of anti-Muslim warriors in *Anandamath*, a novel by nineteenth-century Bengali novelist Bankim Chandra Chatterjee, which explicitly defined Muslims as evil and alien enemies, and British colonial rule as benign and beneficial.

Seeing one's country as a mother may be a benign and comforting image—but using 'Mother India' slogans and songs to disinherit, bully and exclude Muslims defeats that purpose. After all, which mother demands that some of her children keep having to prove their loyalty to her? Why insist that the mother nation requires these tests of loyalty—tests that are especially applied selectively to minorities?

Way back in 1937, Rabindranath Tagore (author of the song that was adopted as India's official anthem) wrote to Subhash Chandra Bose, pointing out that, 'The core of Vande Mataram is a hymn to goddess Durga: this is so plain that there can be no debate about it,' and that, therefore, it would be unreasonable to expect Muslims to view a Hindu deity as the nation and worship her. He concluded, 'The novel *Anandamath* is a work of literature, and so the song is appropriate in it. But Parliament is a place of union for all religious groups, and there the song cannot be appropriate.'[1] Ironically, Tagore, the author of India's national anthem, would fail the loyalty test set by Hindu majoritarian groups. Nearly eighty-two years since Tagore's letter to Bose, we still see the Sangh and BJP, amplified by propagandist TV anchors, insisting that 'Vande Mataram' be played inside the Madhya Pradesh Assembly, and claiming that a refusal to do so amounts to 'anti-national appeasement of Muslims'. The BJP, which raises slogans of 'Vande Mataram' during anti-Muslim pogroms, also raised it while the law criminalizing instant triple talaq was being passed in Parliament.

Not just 'Vande Mataram', even the official national anthem 'Jana Gana Mana' is deployed by communalists as a bullying tool to test the loyalty and patriotism of Muslims and of any and every Indian who is not a supporter of the Sangh's fascist ideology. The funny thing, though, is that the RSS itself is known to viciously oppose 'Jana Gana Mana' and the Indian tricolour.[2] As late as August 2016, RSS leader Bhaiyyaji

Joshi said that 'Vande Mataram' is the real national anthem, while 'Jana Gana Mana' is merely the anthem mandated by the Constitution. Likewise, he said that the saffron flag had been venerated by Indians from time immemorial, while the tricolour was mandated by the Constitution. The tacit implication is that one day the Constitution will be replaced by the *Manusmriti* once India is a Hindu nation, and then 'Jana Gana Mana' will be replaced by 'Vande Mataram' and the tricolour by the saffron flag.[3] In the run-up to the Babri Masjid demolition, Sadhvi Rithambhara's vitriolic speeches attacked 'Jana Gana Mana', declaring that this song was substituted for 'Vande Mataram' only to appease Muslims and secularists.[4] The Sangh abhors 'Jana Gana Mana' because it does not worship the country as divine, and it comprises a diversity of the country's geographical terrain and regions and its 'jana gana' (its people).

A song that can be beautiful and appealing in the anti-colonial freedom struggle can turn ugly and small when someone is forced to raise it as a mark of their (and their community's) defeat, humiliation and subjugation to the Hindu nation, rather than their willing and equal partnership in secular India.

For the Sangh, 'love' and 'worship' of the motherland can only be displayed through hatred for various sections of the people who inhabit the country. There are others who have imagined their country as motherland, without displacing its people from the picture. During the Naxalbari movement, prisoners in jails inscribed a much-loved song on the prison walls: '*Mukt Hobe Priya Matribhumi*' (The Beloved Motherland Will Be Free). That poem expresses a spirit of 'people-first' patriotism—a love for the country that is not the possessive love of the real estate and resources of a country, but rather a love for the people and a desire for *their* liberation. The song ends on this note:

> *Mukt hobe priya matribhumi*
> *Shey din door nei aaj*
> *Mahaan Bharater janata mahaan*
> *Bharat hobe janatar.*

> The beloved motherland will be free,
> That day is not far today!
> See, great India's people are great,
> India will belong to its people!

(Author not known, translation my own)

Such a love isn't expressed in terms of hatred for some *other* nation but in terms of the true liberation of the people of this and all nations. This is exactly how Bhagat Singh and his comrades loved their country—seeking to free its people from colonial bondage and keep it free from the rule of the '*kaale angrez*' (India's own ruling class), while also striving to unite and liberate the working people across the world. Bhagat Singh's dreams of freedom and equality were not confined by national boundaries—he dreamed of a free India in a world free from exploitation and oppression.

An Alternative Politics of Parenting

Whether it is 'Bharat Mata' or 'Gaumata', it seems as though 'mothering', in Indian politics today, is a pretext for violence and hate. In particular, parenting a daughter, in our dominant political discourse, amounts to 'protecting' her from exercising her own autonomy, from loving someone from a prohibited community or gender. And parenting a son, in the same discourse, amounts to training him to hate the people of other communities or countries. Are there other ways in which the love and pain of parenthood figure in Indian politics?

In 1997, when student leader Chandrashekhar (who was a close friend and comrade of mine) was killed at the behest of the criminal don and RJD MP Shahabuddin, his mother Kaushalya Devi led a sustained movement demanding justice.[5] Since 2016, Radhika Vemula has led a struggle to demand justice for her son—Ambedkarite student activist Rohith, who took his own life following persecution by the authorities at Hyderabad University, under pressure from Central government ministers and Sangh leaders. The prime minister, in a vain attempt to quiet the rage that followed Rohith's death, said that he was '*Maa Bharti Ka Laal*' (a beloved son of Mother India)—even as the BJP kept slandering Maa Radhika and her son![6] Fathima Nafees, the mother of JNU student Najeeb (who vanished from the university's campus and is feared to be the victim of a 'disappearance' following a thrashing by a group of ABVP cadres) is also leading an agitation to find her son.[7]

Chanderpati of Haryana has been fighting for justice for her son Manoj who was killed along with his wife, Babli, in Haryana for marrying within the same gotra.[8] The abduction and 'honour killing' of her son Nitish Katara in 2002 turned Neelam Katara into a tireless campaigner against caste-patriarchal crimes against love.[9]

These mothers offer us a politics that restores the humanity and the pain of motherhood. In contrast to the rhetoric about 'Maa Bharti', these women, with the unbearable pain of losing a child, restore to the image of the mother, the love, labour and loss of mothering.

Satya Rani and Shahjahan: Mothers Who Became Sisters in Struggle

In 1979, Satya Rani Chadha's daughter Shashi Bala, married for less than a year, was one of the thousands of young brides who died of 'kitchen stoves bursting' after their parents failed to meet the ever-increasing demands from the husband and in-laws for dowry. Satya Rani knew her daughter had not committed suicide—because Shashi Bala's husband had been threatening to kill his wife if she failed to meet their demands for dowry.[10] In the same year, a woman worker, Shahjahan Apa, also lost her daughter Noorjahan to a dowry killing.[11]

In the massive anti-dowry protests that hit the streets of Delhi in the 1980s, Satya Rani and Shahjahan met— and three years after the deaths of their daughters, they together set up the feminist organization Shakti Shalini to help women facing domestic violence. As Shahjahan Apa puts it, they 'resolved to use the death of [their] daughters as the impetus to fight for the rights of others'.[12]

Shahjahan Apa later said,

In our society, the men get a free servant when they marry, but I believe that men and women are partners in marriage and stand on equal footing. Today our own government betrays us. The police betray us . . . But each day I board the bus that will bring me to our office so that I can meet with the women who have nowhere else to turn. There is a saying in Hindi: *'Meri shakti, meri beti,'* which means, 'My strength is my daughter.'[13]

Our mainstream political discourse is full of shrill slogans about 'saving' daughters and worshipping mothers. Yet, in a country where daughters are considered undesirable and dispensable, how come we hear so little about these two mothers who turned the love for and loss of their daughters into strength offered to other women in need?

A Father's Search for His Son

On 1 March 1976, during the Emergency, Rajan, a young student at REC Calicut (today known as NIT Calicut), in Kerala, was picked up by the police and taken to a detention camp. He then 'disappeared'. His father, a retired Hindi professor T.V. Eachara Varier, began a futile hunt for his son. Ministers, chief ministers, all knew the truth, but none would admit it in front of him. His stubborn struggle eventually unearthed the truth: Rajan had died in police custody following brutal torture.

Rajan had been arrested as a 'Naxalite', with no evidence linking him to any crime. His story became synonymous with the Emergency and its attack on civil liberties and human rights. He was subjected to a particularly brutal form of torture known as *uruttal* (rolling) in which a heavy wooden log would be rolled over the thighs followed by kicking in the stomach by a police officer with heavy boots.

Professor Varier wrote a book about his experience of searching for his son. He described the way in which Rajan's mother (who became insane) never stopped expecting her son to return. He ended the book with an account of a visit to the Kakkayam detention camp where his son was tortured and killed. His final words leave the reader with a question and a challenge:

> I still have no answer to the question of whether or not I feel vengeance. But I leave a question to the world: why are you making my innocent child stand in the rain even after his death?
>
> I don't close the door. Let the rain lash inside and drench me. Let at least my invisible son know that his father never shut the door.[14]

Rajan's father wrote, 'I should not leave the new generation to that wooden bench and the rolling.'[15] Those words should shame and haunt us today because brutal torture—including the *uruttal* torture—continues even today in our police stations. These forms of torture were not an 'excess' of the Emergency—they are part of casual, everyday routine policing in India. For the poor, for the Dalits, Adivasis and minorities, every day is an 'emergency', irrespective of who is in power.

In 2018, again in Kerala, sixty-seven-year-old single mother Prabhavathi Amma succeeded in winning the conviction of the policemen who had performed the same brutal rolling torture on her son Udayakumar, a scrap collector, thirteen years ago. Udayakumar was picked up by the police on charges of petty theft and killed under custodial torture. Prabhavathi said their family was so poor that they never had the money to get a photograph taken of Udayakumar; the only picture she has of her son is of his dead body. When a special CBI court convicted the police officers for her son's custodial killing, Prabhavathi said exactly what Varier had said decades ago: 'I should do this for my son, so that no other mother will have to go through what I went through.'[16]

These fathers and mothers lost everything when their sons were taken, tortured and killed—they struggled so that others should be spared the same fate. Our callous tolerance of custodial torture, as a society, lets down these parents. It is even more obscene that such custodial torture is rationalized as 'national security' and 'protecting the motherland', and the voices arguing in favour of the principles of human rights and civil liberties are vilified as 'anti-national'.

When Women's Autonomy Is 'Anti-National'

Autonomy for girls and women means the freedom to wander around in public spaces, make friends and hang out with them, fall in and out of love, make decision for themselves and explore their full selves.

But for Adivasi girls and women of Bastar, where the 'war on Maoists' is the pretext for extreme militarization in civilian areas, their very autonomy and mobility are cited

as alibis to defend police and paramilitary forces accused
of rape and murder. For them, the police and paramilitary
do not represent 'security', they represent arbitrary, cruel
power and terror that can rape or kill with total impunity.

Take the case of Meena Khalko, a fifteen-year-old
girl from the Oraon Adivasi tribe who lived in the remote
village of Karcha in Balrampur district, Chhattisgarh.
Meena grazed goats and was a familiar figure on her
bicycle. She was friends with a truck driver whom she
would meet near a river close to her village. One evening in
2011, she left home on her bicycle, telling her parents she
was visiting her friend. Her parents never saw her again.
The next morning, they were summoned to the hospital,
to find their daughter dead. The police claimed she was
a Maoist who had been killed in an 'encounter' near the
neighbouring village of Nawadih.[17]

Meena's parents, Buddheshwar and Guttiyari, as well
as all the people of Karcha, were absolutely sure she was no
Maoist. The people of Nawadih also strongly countered
police claims that there had been any prolonged gunfire
indicating an encounter near their village. The postmortem
report showed sperm in Meena's body. The villagers were
all sure Meena had been raped and killed by the police,
who then claimed she had been killed in an encounter.
The government and the police insisted the encounter was
genuine—and yet, compensated Meena's family with cash
and a job for her brother. If the encounter was genuine,
why was the government paying compensation? If it was
an attempt at hush money, Meena's parents refused to be
hushed.

Four years later, a judicial commission established that the villagers were right. Meena had been raped and murdered, and the killing had then been staged as an encounter. The commission noted that 'blood clots were found in her lungs and intestines on account of cuts. The seventh rib is fractured. This shows that intercourse was done using physical force on Ms Meena Khalko.'[18]

Soon after Meena's death (long before the judicial commission submitted its findings vindicating Meena), the state government had repeated a familiar script in the state assembly to maintain that Meena was killed in an encounter. When opposition leaders had alleged that Meena had been raped and killed, the state's home minister, Nankiram Kanwar, of the BJP, asked why Meena had left home in the evening: girls who do not stay home in the evenings are bad girls, everyone knows that! He added, for good measure, that the forensic report indicated that Meena was 'habitual at sex'.[19]

It was not the first time an Adivasi girl's rape by policemen was being dismissed with the insinuation that she was habituated to sex and that her sexual autonomy and mobility provided an alibi for the accused. In 1972, another Adivasi teenager, Mathura, had been raped by a policeman at a police station. An infamous 1978 Supreme Court verdict upheld the sessions court's finding that Mathura was a 'shocking liar': a two-finger test[20] had claimed her to be 'habituated to sex', so the courts assumed she must have consented to sex with the policeman.[21] This judgment was challenged by an open letter to the chief justice of India by four professors of law, sparking off a sustained feminist

movement that demanded, and won, some improvements
in the rape law's understanding of consent.[22]

Meena Khalko's story reminds us that for Adivasi
teenagers raped by policemen, their sexual history and their
mobility and autonomy continue to be used to justify their
rape by the police. Kanwar's remarks in the Chhattisgarh
Assembly implied that a girl who could tell her parents
she was bicycling off to meet her friend, who was friends
with a truck driver, could not ever be raped. A girl who
is habituated to sex must also be habitually anti-national:
how outrageous to accuse the 'nationalist' police force in a
conflict area, fighting for Mother India, of raping a Naxal
slut who was anyway habituated to sex?

In the Sangh's and BJP's political imagination, women's
sexual autonomy is often linked with being anti-national.
This is why a 'dossier' on the 'anti-national' activities
supposedly rife on the Jawaharlal Nehru University campus
displayed an obsessive and prurient fascination for the
sex lives of the students. It is why, in television debates
(ironically, on sexual harassment) and on Twitter, BJP's
Rajya Sabha MP Subramanian Swamy has repeatedly
resorted to dissing my arguments by proclaiming that
I am a 'Marxist–Leninist/Naxalite who has free sex'.[23]
A JNU faculty member offered an insight into why sexual
autonomy is seen by the Sangh as anti-national:

By not incarcerating women, by having a GSCASH,
by relentlessly struggling for a gender-plural campus
free of surveillance and policing, universities like JNU
challenge not only patriarchy, but also its chief clients:

caste and exclusionary religion. It should therefore be no surprise to any student as to why from the Sanghistanian perspective, at least some normal young people look like they have already seceded from a nation built on the hegemonies of caste [Brahminism], religion [Hinduism] and gender [antiquated Male, size 56].[24]

But while JNU students and those like me can laugh off this Sanghi fear of sexually and politically 'free' women, this political imagination has far more grim consequences for girls and women in conflict areas, like Meena Khalko.

Buddheshwar and Guttiyari have had to suffer the pain of their daughter being raped and killed—and then having the home minister dignify her assailants as nationalists and demean her as an anti-national slut. Buddheshwar, speaking to a journalist, said, '*Humri dil ko bahut kadta hai* [It hurts my heart a lot].' Stretching his hands a foot apart, he said, 'My heart was once this big,' adding, 'it's this small now,' with his fingers an inch apart.[25]

'Beti Bachao'—from 'Security Forces'?

Meena Khalko's story is by no means an exception. In a conflict area like Bastar, such experiences are the norm. Even the daily work and play of girls and boys in this region are fraught with the danger of arbitrary arrest or custodial killing.

In 2015, for instance, three Adivasi women, Somdi, Gangi and Lakme filed a complaint with a magistrate about their teenage daughters being chased, beaten, made to march 21 km away and then illegally detained overnight. The three girls had left home together to graze their buffaloes and bathe in the river, just a kilometre away from their village. When they spotted a large group of police and Central Reserve Police Force (CRPF) men emerging from the nearby forest, they turned around and ran back home. The men from the special task force of Chhattisgarh police and the CRPF chased them into their homes, dragged them out, beat them up and made them walk for eight hours to the Kukanar police station 21 km away where they were detained overnight. Their mothers and aunts who tried to follow them and ask the police why they were being taken away, were beaten black and blue. The girls were produced before a magistrate the next day and kept in an observation home 400 km away.

The police interpreted the girls' presence in the open spaces, and their response of fleeing at the sight of the police as a suspicious sign of their guilt, saying, 'Why did the girls run? Obviously, they were guilty of something. Why were they in the forest? Only "*sandigdh log*" [suspicious persons] roam around in the forest.'[26]

In 2016, I was a part of a fact-finding team that visited Bastar. We broke up into groups and visited remote villages, following up on newspaper reports of encounter killings.[27]

A news item in the *Dainik Bhaskar*[28] dated 31 January 2016, with the headline 'Two Fleeing Naxalites Fall in Ditch, Killed by Police', quoted the police as claiming that two armed women Maoists, Vanjam Shanti and Siriyam Pojje, were killed when they fell into a ditch during an hour-long gun battle on 30 January 2016. The newspaper carried a photograph of the bodies, which gave every appearance of the two being very young girls, dressed not in Maoist uniforms but saris. Members of our team visited Palamadgu village in Dornapal tehsil, Sukma district, where the encounter had supposedly taken place. The team found that Shanti was thirteen years old and Pojje, fourteen. They were teenagers, not adult women and let alone armed Maoists. One of our team members who had made it to this village said that Vanjam Aade, mother of Shanti, could barely speak through her tears. She said that Shanti and Pojje had gone early that morning to release the hens (who were kept cooped up at night to safeguard them from wild animals) and then have a bath in the river. This was what the girls did each morning. And at 8 a.m., Aade was told by villagers that her daughter had been shot dead.[29]

And it is not only girls whose lives are in such danger in Bastar; young boys and men are also very vulnerable to completely unprovoked attacks, arrests and even murder at the hands of 'security' forces. At Arlampalli village in Sukma on 3 November 2015, three friends, Vetti Lacchu (nineteen), Sodhi Muya (twenty-one) and Dudhi Bhima (twenty-three), had done what young men do—go out for a drink together. As they headed back, they were accosted by the police and beaten up. As one of them fled, he was shot dead, and the other two were made to carry the body of their friend to a pick-up van, after which they too were shot dead. All three were later branded 'Maoists'.[30]

Herding goats and buffaloes, going to meet a boyfriend, having a bath in the river, hanging out with friends, dancing at a harvest festival—for Bastar's kids, these comfortingly

ordinary everyday things are done under the shadow of
the police and paramilitary guns; and for Bastar's parents,
the fear of losing a child to arbitrary violence is a constant
companion.

The Mothers of Manipur

In July 2004, twelve Manipuri women turned mothers' hurt
and rage into a new and raw kind of political protest. These
women, calling themselves 'imas' (mothers), assembled in
a flash protest outside the Assam Rifles headquarters at
Kangla Fort in Manipur. Stripping themselves naked, they
held up a banner that challenged the Indian armed forces:
'Indian Army Rape Us.' With furious tears in their eyes,
their voices cracking, they shouted, 'We are all Manorama's
mothers, come, rape us!' And 'Down with AFSPA!' People
watching them at the spot and later on local television
channels, could not restrain their tears. All of Manipur
erupted in sustained protest demanding the scrapping of
the Armed Forces (Special Powers) Act (AFSPA).

Who was Manorama? What is the AFSPA? What
had made these mothers of Manipur issue a challenge that
was at such odds with the romanticized myth of chivalrous
armed forces protecting Mother India?

Five days before the protest, a paramilitary contingent,
the 17th Assam Rifles, barged into the east Imphal home
of a young Manipuri woman, Thangjam Manorama. They
dragged her into the courtyard, tortured and molested her,
and took her away with them claiming she was a militant.
Two hours later, they claimed they had had to shoot at

her legs to prevent her from escaping, and that she died of her injuries.

The problem with this tale was that there were bullet holes in Manorama's genitals, and her body bore the unmistakable signs of torture. Her mother and brothers testified to the fact that she had been molested and tortured in their own home before she was taken away. When women saw Manorama's body, brutalized, they felt impelled to do something out of the ordinary to protest. Many of these women had been active in *meira paibi* (women torchbearer) groups that had mobilized on various social issues in Manipur. Keeping their plan a secret even from their own family members, these women went to the Kangla Fort wearing nothing but their outer garments, which they then stripped off in protest.

The mothers of Manipur were not protesting just that one act of rape and murder: they were challenging the draconian AFSPA, which ensures that armed forces cannot be prosecuted for murder on the pretext that any violence by such forces must be presumed to be 'in pursuit of their duty'. It was this Act, they felt, which emboldened the armed forces in Manipur to rape and kill with the confidence that there would be no consequences. When rape and murder are cloaked in the uniforms of 'nationalism', when Indian nationalism is made to feel like an oppressive colonial occupation that treats entire nationalities worse than prisoners of war, is it any surprise at all that women protesting it feel repelled by that nationalism? Ima Nganbi, one of the twelve women who participated in the naked protest, said she remembers celebrating India's independence day as a child, but no longer wants to sing the national anthem, or stand up, when it is played.[31]

Under pressure from the protests in Manipur, the state government set up a judicial commission headed by C. Upendra Singh, retired district and sessions judge, in 2004, to probe Manorama's killing. The commission completed its probe in November 2004, despite unceasing obstructions from the Assam Rifles, which claimed that the AFSPA shielded it from any such probe. The Assam Rifles and the Central government have consistently blocked every attempt to act on the findings and recommendations of the Justice Upendra Commission.

The Justice Upendra Commission concluded without any room for doubt that Manorama had been subjected to 'brutal and merciless torture' by the 17th Assam Rifles personnel.[32] With Manorama 'clutching on to her mother, Khumanleima', she was dragged out to the verandah screaming 'Ima, Ima, Khamu (mother, mother, please stop them)'.[33] Manorama's brother, Basu, had seen his sister subjected to waterboarding torture. He also saw a member of the arresting party inserting a kitchen knife under his sister's underwear, pulling down her *phanek* (skirt) and pulling up her T-shirt to expose her body. Later, she was made to change her clothes before being taken away by the contingent.

The Commission concluded that:

> The contention of the Assam Rifles that victim Manorama was shot at her legs while she was running in order to escape from the custody of the 17th Assam Rifles is a naked lie . . . most of the injuries reveal that

they were shot while the victim was in prone, while lying, bending positions with an intention to kill and even after she was in helpless condition.[34]

It also concluded that:

The evidence and circumstances clearly indicate that victim Manorama might have been subject to rape and sexual harassment. The arresting team of the Assam Rifles with a view to cover up the crime over the person of the victim, had specifically fired on genital organ . . . this aspect exposes not only barbaric attitude but also their attempt to fabricate false evidence with a view to cover up the offence committed by them.[35]

Why are the voices of the mothers of Manipur silenced in the name of honouring Mother India? If Jyoti Singh Pandey, brutally raped and killed on a bus in Delhi in 2012, could be seen as 'India's daughter', why is Thangjam Manorama, victim of a far more cold-blooded, planned, ruthless rape and murder, not seen as India's daughter? Why do only Manipur's *meira paibis* see her as their daughter?

In 2004, I visited Manipur not long after the anti-AFSPA agitation. I recall that when we met Khumanleima, she would not even meet our eyes. Her grief and shock were so great that she could not even respond to anyone's words or gestures. The *meira paibi* became the voice for the pain that Manorama's own mother could not then express.

There is something else I remember from that visit. On 6 October 2004, we landed in Imphal airport, to realize

that the 'godman' Sri Sri Ravishankar (of the 'Art of Living'
fame) had travelled on the same flight as us. His stated
purpose, we learned, was to bring 'peace' to Manipur. I
recall my shock at seeing him greeted at the airport and
escorted by a team of Assam Rifles personnel—the same
Assam Rifles that was defending its men accused of raping
and murdering Manorama. During his visit, Ravishankar
preached 'peace' to Manipur's protesting people—but
never visited Manorama's mother or asked the Central
government why it was allowing the Assam Rifles to
practise the 'art of killing and raping'. He seemed to be
brokering a 'peace' divorced from justice, as an agent of the
force responsible for the violence and the impunity.

I ended my report[36] on that visit to Manipur by recalling
the Manipuri play *Draupadi* by the renowned playwright of
Manipur, Ojas Heisnam Kanhailal. That play was in turn
inspired by the central character in Mahasweta Devi's story
'Dopdi', a Santhal woman who is picked up as a 'Naxalite'
and raped by the police. Instead of being browbeaten,
however, Dopdi confronts her oppressors, naked and
bleeding, and challenges them to 'counter (encounter)
me', even as they are struck with fear at her challenge.
Kanhailal's play had been performed since the year 2000,
and actress Sabitri Heisnam, in its final scenes, would
disrobe on stage, asking the rapist soldiers to 'counter' her.
Through that play, fiction seemed to have anticipated fact.
Like Mahasweta's Dopdi and Kanhailal's Draupadi, these
mothers of Manipur defiantly disrobed themselves—and
in the process, pulled the patriotic robes off the atrocities
by the armed forces.

Parents in Eternal Limbo

Rajan's parents, waiting endlessly to know what happened to their son, became the emblem of the Emergency. In Kashmir, there are literally thousands of such parents, waiting in vain for word of their sons, abducted by the armed forces.

One such parent is Parveena Ahanger. I met her in November 2016, when I visited the Kashmir Valley as part of a solidarity team with members from people's movements all over India. She told us the story she has repeated many times over for nearly three decades. Her son, Javaid Ahmad, was a student of Class XI in 1990 when he was picked up by paramilitary forces from Batamaloo. 'I kept waiting for him to return, thinking he's innocent, they can't keep him for long, they will question him and then let him go,' she said. Then, she approached the courts, then politicians and the government—to no avail. She then began keeping clippings from a newspaper that would print lists of 'disappeared' persons. For years, she travelled the length and breadth of the Valley, visiting remote villages to track down other parents of persons who had disappeared after being picked up by the Indian military and paramilitary forces. That was how she formed the Association of Parents of Disappeared Persons (APDP)—a platform of Kashmiri parents of people who had disappeared under mysterious circumstances. Parveena told us that for her and other parents like her, life was like living forever in a limbo, never knowing if their beloved sons (or brothers or husbands) were alive or dead. Once or twice every month, these parents gather at Parveena's home, and then march from there to hold some kind of protest demonstration—defying the prohibitions on almost every kind of protest, however peaceful and however small in the Valley.

According to Parveena, at least 8000 people in Kashmir are estimated to have disappeared after being picked up by Indian forces. What happened to these people? In 2009, human rights groups, including the APDP, prepared a report on 2700 'unknown, unmarked, and mass graves' in fifty-five villages in three districts—Bandipora, Baramulla and Kupwara—of north Kashmir. Most of the graves contained unnamed bodies, and a large number of graves contained multiple (more than one, and in some cases up to seventeen) bodies.[37] The APDP and other rights groups believe that most of the bodies in the mass graves are of victims of disappearances and custodial killings. When people picked up by the forces die in custody, they are buried in unmarked graves, without taking the trouble to inform their parents, so that the custodial force can be spared any explanations. The State Human Rights Commission of Kashmir ordered a DNA probe into the mass graves in 2017—but the parents are still waiting for this order to be followed. A woman whose husband disappeared in 2002 told a journalist that she and others like her wanted 'emotional closure': 'We want to know whether our family members are buried in these graves. At least, we will get an address to mourn.'[38]

What the APDP does in Kashmir, mothers and fathers have done in other parts of the world, where military dictatorships have 'disappeared' people and robbed parents of their offspring. In Argentina, during the US-backed military dictatorship (1976–83), mothers of disappeared persons began to defy the regime's bans on protests and gather at the Plaza de Mayo in Buenos Aires.[39] To convey that mothers would always remember the babyhood of their adult offspring, they would wear white scarves on their heads to symbolize diapers. These women were referred to by the regime as '*las locas*' (madwomen). But the government found the 'madwomen' dangerous enough to 'disappear' many of them. In 2005, the remains of three of the leading mothers of the Plaza de Mayo—Azucena Villaflor, Esther Careaga and María Eugenia Bianco—who had themselves been 'disappeared' in 1977, were identified in an unmarked grave.[40] CoMadres is a similar organization of mothers whose sons and daughters were abducted by a dictatorial regime in El Salvador. A 1987 song titled 'Mothers of the Disappeared', by the Irish rock band U2 and their lead singer Bono is a tribute to the mothers of the Plaza de Mayo and CoMadres who hear the heartbeat and see the tears of the sons and daughters who were taken from them at midnight.[41]

In Chile, too, women would gather in the capital, Santiago, to protest the disappearances of their loved ones, at the behest of the dictatorial regime of Augusto Pinochet.[42] These Chilean women would dance the *cueca*, the national dance of Chile that is usually danced in couples, alone—holding a photograph of their loved one. In 1987, the English singer Sting composed 'They Dance Alone' in memory of these women who by 'dancing with the missing . . . dancing with the dead . . . dancing with their fathers . . . dancing with their sons' kept an accusing finger pointed at the brutal Pinochet regime.[43]

Writing in December 1999, the Uruguayan writer Eduardo Galeano asked, 'What would it be like if we began to exercise the never proclaimed right to dream? What if we raved without constraints for a while?' And as part of this utopia he dreamed of, Galeano said, 'In Argentina, the Locas de la Plaza de Mayo (madwomen of the Plaza de Mayo) will be held up as examples of mental health, because during the time of obligatory amnesia they refused to forget.'[44] As Indian citizens, we have a choice. We can either help our governments and our media enforce the 'obligatory amnesia' about the terrible crimes committed in the name of India—in our name. Or we can be 'mad' enough to join Parveena Ahanger and the parents in APDP in challenging this obligatory amnesia. The parents can never forget, and the least we can do is to do them the favour of letting them remind us.

Autonomy—as Women, as Communities

Women, in every community in India, face patriarchal restrictions on their autonomy. But when their community itself faces severe, violent militarizations that restrict its own autonomy *as a community*, it becomes much more challenging for women to assert their own autonomy. Some of the most inspiring assertions of women's autonomy under these challenging circumstances come from Kashmir.

In the summer of 2017, newspapers carried photographs of Kashmiri schoolgirls pelting stones at armed forces. In one of the most iconic of these photos, a schoolgirl could be seen with a football in one hand, pelting a stone with the other.[45] It emerged later that these girls were part of a football team, walking to the playground with their coach. When a policeman 'mistook them for stone pelters' and slapped one of them, the girls picked up stones and hurled them at the cops. Essar Batool, Kashmiri feminist activist and writer, observed, that 'these images of young women with their cute bunny bags or football in hand are extremely powerful. They shatter many myths and stereotypes about Kashmiri women.' Batool felt that for the Kashmiri schoolgirls, picking up a stone was 'about feeling empowered', a way of challenging 'not only the political regime but also patriarchal norms within which women have been subjugated'.[46]

Nearly a decade ago, in 2010, filmmaker Sanjay Kak had already remarked on the significance of Kashmiri women stepping out of traditional roles to directly confront and defy the Indian state's armed forces. He commented on the presence of the ordinary middle-aged Kashmiri woman in the protests, 'dressed in ordinary salwar-kameez, pastel pink, baby blue, purple and yellow', her head 'casually covered with a dupatta', seeming to be 'unconcerned about being recognized', and carrying a stone in her hand ready to fling at security forces. What put that stone in her hand? Kak wrote that 'this is no ordinary anger, but an old, bottled-up rage, gathered over so many years that it has settled, and turned rock hard. That accumulated fury is the stone in her hand.'[47]

Batool was one of the six young Kashmiri women in their twenties, who during the protests that followed the Delhi 2012 gangrape, began to revisit the Kunan Poshpora rape case of 1991, in which thirty-one women of Kunan and Poshpora villages were gang-raped by Indian armed forces during a night raid. They wrote about that experience, documenting the narratives of the women who survived that rape and still fight for justice, in a book titled *Do You Remember Kunan Poshpora?*[48]

Natasha Rather, one of the co-authors of that book, addressed a conference of my organization as a guest in November 2016, and offered insights into the burden of 'honour' that links the struggles of Kashmiri women and those of women in India and South Asia more generally:

> In 1991, and even now, it is not easy for women to speak of rape or anything 'sexual' in Kashmiri society. We just heard Neelam-ji [Neelam Katara] speak about women facing violence in the name of 'honour'. We know how women in every section of South Asian society are made to bear the burden of honour. Whether we like it or not, we women are forced to uphold the honour of our husbands, fathers, brothers or sons. And if we fail to maintain that honour, we are blamed. It is this honour that the Indian Army soldiers targeted at Kunan Poshpora and other places. When you 'disappear' Kashmiri men in extra-judicial killings, when you detain and torture them, you are targeting their bodies and their spirit as individuals. But when you target women, you are targeting their entire families, their entire community. What the women of Kunan Poshpora showed was that by targeting women to attack the 'honour' of the struggling people, you cannot wound their spirit.[49]

During our visit to a village in Kashmir in November 2016, a group of women and girls told us about an attack on their village. Most of the women spoke only Kashmiri, so a Class IV schoolgirl, Muskan, stepped forward to speak to us in Hindi.[50] Looking us boldly in the eye, she told us, '*Army wale Eid ke din hamari behanon ke baal pakad kar ghaseet kar le gaye. Ek mahila behosh ho gayi. Army wale hans rahe the, hame laga ki woh hamari izzat loot lenge isliye ham bhag gaye.*' (On the day of Eid, armymen came and dragged our sisters by the hair. One woman fainted. The armymen were laughing. We thought they will rape us, so we ran away.)

I asked her if she had ever joined the protests, and if so, why. Without a moment's shyness or hesitation she replied, '*Han hum andolan karte hain. Hum Modi se kehte hain Kashmir se nikal jao. Hum azadi chahte hain. Hum Mehbooba Mufti se kehte hain gaddi chhor do.*' (Yes, we agitate. We tell Modi to get out of Kashmir. We want freedom. And we tell Mehbooba she must quit her chair.)

On an Aaj Tak show[51] about rape threats to a Delhi University student, the BJP spokesperson Sambit Patra declared me '*deshdrohi*' (anti-national) because 'she says army men can rape'. Repeatedly raising long-drawn-out slogans of 'Vande Mataram', which he asked the studio audience (of journalism students) to join, Patra instigated an ABVP cadre in the audience to ask me to declare whether or not I considered Kashmir to be an integral part of India. A debate that was supposed to be about rape threats, turned into a test of 'nationalism' and 'loyalty' for a women's rights activist, the show's sole woman panelist![52] Likewise, Arnab Goswami on the Republic ran a show haranguing the left with the hashtag #LeftInsultsArmy, about the remarks of a left leader against the draconian nature of AFSPA, which is used as a shield for rape and murder.[53]

As I pointed out on the show, if criticizing the Army's impunity from charges of rape and murder amounts to 'insulting the Army', the Supreme Court itself is insulting the Army by demanding accountability from it for no less than 1528 extrajudicial killings and instances of rape in Manipur. The Supreme Court judges slammed the attorney general with these brutally harsh words for the Army:

> Do you have people in Army who rape? It is an alleged gangrape in uniform—an aggravated form of crime . . . Here is a thirteen-year-old girl who worked in a rubber farm. There was no allegation that she was an insurgent. Two people come and rape her. She narrates her ordeal to her mother and a sister and then commits suicide. Have you [state government] decided that let Army come and rape anyone, what can we do?[54]

When 700 Army officers filed a petition suggesting that such remarks by Supreme Court judges had a 'demoralizing' effect on the armed forces, the court responded that surely the armed forces are made of 'sterner stuff' and the apprehension that they have been demoralized 'is suggestive of a weakness in them'.[55] Why should it be an 'insult' to the armed forces to be held accountable to India's Constitution and international conventions? After all, it is the military dictatorships that boast of being immune to human rights standards and international conventions: surely it is a far greater insult to the armed forces of a democratic India to *fail* to hold them accountable?

On 5 August 2019, the Modi government abrogated Article 370, which was a move towards stripping Jammu and Kashmir of statehood and autonomy. Subsequently, many in the government claimed that the move was necessary to liberate Kashmiri women from patriarchal oppression.[56] I visited the Valley with other activists and concerned people just days after 5 August, and it was under total lockdown. We had asked girls and women what they felt about these claims that the government sought to liberate them. This question was met with angry retorts such as this one: 'Who will liberate us? The BJP leaders who are saying men in UP or Haryana (where the sex ratio is low) can now source fair brides from Kashmir? Are we apples or peaches of Kashmir—goods to be looted by our conquerors?'[57]

These girls and women were referring to a statement by Haryana Chief Minister Manohar Lal Khattar in the wake of the abrogation of Article 370. Khattar had said that Haryana had a poor sex ratio, forcing men to 'source' brides from other states like Bihar. He said, 'People are saying that doors of Kashmir have been opened and we can get girls from there.'[58] Not long before him, a BJP MLA from Khatauli in Muzaffarnagar, UP, said his (male) party workers were excited because they could now 'marry the fair girls of Kashmir'.[59] There has been a flurry of pop songs urging Indian men to travel to Kashmir to claim the land and women.[60] Such rhetoric is redolent of colonial conquest, fantasizing about the sexual conquest of women as the spoils of war. And these fantasies have a real-life impact on women. People of several villages in Kashmir told reporters that soldiers raiding their homes at night had not only indulged in torture and loot, they had 'threatened to take away and marry their female relatives'. One man said he had sent his daughter away to a safer place because soldiers would come repeatedly to his home looking for his daughter. Another added, 'They're marauding our homes and hearths like a victorious army.'[61]

In previous chapters, we've seen how parents, communities, even courts, often take decisions for women against their will, claiming that women cannot be expected to know what's best for them. 'We are curtailing your liberties for your own good' is a sentiment with which women in India are very familiar. Similar arguments are now being given to justify the caging of Kashmir.

In a piece in the *Washington Post*, an Indian journalist wrote that in 2016, a less-than-strict curfew allowed protests to take place, costing the lives of thirty-seven protesters in the first week.[62] She then quoted a spokesperson for the Indian government's administration in Kashmir, who said, 'to protect lives, some liberties may have to be compromised'.[63] Kashmiri civilians have lost their lives in protests because the forces are empowered to use pellet guns and bullets against them.[64] The lockdown endangered lives by jeopardizing access to medical care.[65] Earlier in this book, we have seen that women are not safer when they are less free. The curtailment of freedom itself is never 'protection', but one of the worst forms of violence.

When I think of Kashmir, I do not think of a piece of real estate, but of the living, breathing people there—people who are an 'integral part of humanity'. When I think about Kashmir, I remember Muskan—that bold, brave girl who was asserting her own autonomy and that of her people.

CONCLUSION

Towards Fearless Freedom

> You write in order to change the world, knowing perfectly well that you probably can't, but also knowing that literature is indispensable to the world . . . The world changes according to the way people see it, and if you alter, even but a millimeter the way people look at reality, then you can change it.
>
> —James Baldwin[1]

> *Kal ka geet liye honthon par, aaj ladaai jaari hai* [With tomorrow's song on our lips, we fight today's battles]
>
> —Maheshwar[2]

In December 2012 and January 2013, the anti-rape movement that swept Delhi heard bold cries demanding 'Fearless Freedom', and also demanding *'naari mukti, sabki mukti'* (freedom for women, freedom for all).

Women (and indeed all of us—women, LGBTQIA persons, men) can be fully free only when humanity is free—and that, as I see it, will need us to throw off the yoke of the entire oppressive, exploitative structure. It will, in other words, need a revolution, a complete change in the way human beings stand in relation to each other and to nature.

What is the point of imagining a revolutionized world free of all hierarchies; it is not going to be a reality in our lifetime, I am often asked.

Revolutionary goals are like a compass on a long march—it may take very long to reach the destination, and the destination may not be in sight, but a compass makes sure we march in the right direction and do not lose our way.

If you are putting together a thousand-piece jigsaw puzzle, you can do it only with the full picture clear in your head. Without the full picture, you cannot connect the little pieces to each other.

We need to keep tomorrow's song on our lips in today's battles—and that is what gives meaning and direction to today's battles. We need to hope and work for the day that all women and all of humanity shall be free, and all hierarchies shall be history—and it is then that we are able to see today's struggles whole, rather than as piecemeal and disconnected from each other.

Revolutionary goals are not empty dreams made up of nice ideas. Revolutionary dreams are rooted firmly in the earth—and humans working together can make those dreams come to life on this earth. With that revolutionary destination firmly in our sights, we are able to recognize how each of the less distant goals we seek for ourselves, cannot be achieved without a struggle for women's autonomy at their core.

Autonomy is not about a mere 'choice' made by an individual—it isn't like choosing between various brands at a supermarket. Autonomy in a feminist sense is necessarily autonomy—to whatever extent possible—*from social and economic structures*, and it is *never* autonomy for oneself to hurt the rights and liberties of other women, other oppressed people.

I have in mind Prachi Trivedi, one of the protagonists of the 2012 documentary film by Nisha Pahuja, *The World Before Her*.[3] Prachi is a young woman, a trainer at a Durga Vahini camp, in which young girls from rural India are taught to wield weapons and hate Muslims. Prachi's father, a VHP leader, once burnt her foot, to punish her for lying—but Prachi says it's okay for him to do that, since he allowed her to live, rather than be killed at birth like so many other baby girls in India. Prachi is not conventionally feminine, she says she wishes she had been born neither a girl nor a boy, and she is not interested in getting married, but she accepts that her father will take that decision for her. The thrill that women in the Durga Vahini camp get from wielding weapons, raising slogans and learning martial arts moves is all circumscribed by an ideology that tells them women must be subservient to men; that women's purpose is to give birth; and that women are required to step out of domestic roles and be battle-ready only to 'save' the country from Muslims—i.e., to inflict violence on minorities. This is not feminist autonomy. A young woman like Prachi, who joins the Durga Vahini, experiences, briefly, what may feel like a taste of liberty—but she's 'allowed' that autonomy by a patriarchal father and a fascist organization only so that she can hate and inflict violence on Muslim minorities.

The same film also follows young women who are participants in a Miss India beauty pageant. Does the world of the beauty pageant offer autonomy? The young women's bodies are subjected to Botox and to humiliating tests (such as when all their faces are covered to allow judges to judge the beauty of their legs alone). The pageant encourages every woman to compete fiercely with other women—each is out for her own. And yet the pageant not only disallows mutual solidarity, it also erases individuality: so much so that a contestant's own mother is unable to recognize her daughter in the line-up of contestants who all look the same![4]

Both the Durga Vahini camp and the beauty pageant boot camp offer young women what can pass for 'empowerment'. But both demand a measure of self-hate: the Vahini wants women to internalize a brutal patriarchy and become its agents, while the Miss India pageant wants women to internalize the notion that 'beauty' requires their bodies to be subjected to all sorts of 'corrections', indignities and humiliations. In addition, of course, the Vahini camp requires young girls and women to learn to hate Muslim men and women, and trains them to attack the autonomy of other Hindu women who may love or marry a Muslim!

To wrest autonomy from oppressive and exploitative structures calls for collective struggles, for drawing strength from each other, not in competition with each other. That's why a feminist quest for autonomy cannot be about a few individual women 'breaking the glass ceiling' in competition with a handful of other men and women. A recently published *Feminism for the 99 Per Cent: A Manifesto* asserts, 'We have no interest in breaking the glass ceiling, while leaving the majority of women to clean up the shards.'[5]

In Indian traditions of art, we have the wonderful image of the Abhisarika—the woman who braves all sorts of dangers to venture out into the stormy night, through forests full of snakes, to meet her lover. Comparing the women who came out with candles and torches to march against rape in Delhi in December 2012 to Abhisarika, Shuddhabrata Sengupta wrote that Abhisarika was always seen as a source of light:

> Her desire is a flame that lights up everything around her. In the folk songs of Punjab, she can be a firefly, a restless, wandering *jugni*. And women, together, out on the streets, out to claim each hour, each watch of the night, can light up an entire forest of a city with their flickering, blazing fire.[6]

We need women to be Abhisarika today: with their desires—for lovers, yes, but also for the simple pleasure of a walk on the street or a cup of a chai at a street corner, for reading and research, for adventure, for wanderlust, for andolans, for revolution—to light up everything around them. And when many women become Abhisarika, the streets and the dark nights will be much safer. Imagine a woman alone on the street at night—and we imagine danger; but imagine a street full of women going about their own business and pleasure, and to women, such a street immediately seems safe!

These Abhisarikas can change the ways in which we imagine and shape our relationships, our society, our families, our movements. Instead of worrying about proving they are a 'good' (obedient) rather than 'bad' (disobedient) daughter, sister, or partner/spouse, they can find ways of feeling comfortable and confident in their autonomous skin without the need to seek permission and validation for that autonomy. Older women can be Abhisarika too—they can respect their own autonomy and that of younger women and girls in their own households.

If you're a mother or a parent, you may ask, 'It is all very well to speak of "fearless freedom", but, of course, my daughter is going to feel fear in a world where sexual violence is so rampant.' Well, yes, but you do have it in your power as a parent to free your daughter of the fear that speaking up about sexual harassment or violence will mean that *you* will curtail her education. That in itself would be a huge step towards giving your daughter the gift of fearless freedom. Likewise, you could free your child (of any gender) of the fear that coming out to their parents as lesbian or gay or trans could lose them your love and acceptance.

We can, in fact we must, put women's autonomy at the centre of our struggles against fascism, against capitalism, against Brahmanism, against patriarchy and against heteronormativity. We can unlearn the habit deeply ingrained even in women of dividing ourselves up into 'good' and 'bad' women. At home, at work, in our communities and neighbourhoods, we can find ways to enable ourselves and other women to organize, to campaign, to find support and solidarity, and to fight.

Will this book change the world? Perhaps not. But if it can even alter by a millimetre how you and I look at women's autonomy and autonomous women—if we can begin to admire and cherish women's *bekhauf azaadi*, their *veera sutantiram*, their fearless freedom—perhaps we *can* change the world!

AFTERWORD

Dear reader,

If you have stayed with me on this journey till here, thank you.

You know that this book is an elaboration of the core slogan of the 2012–13 anti-rape movement in India. This movement demanded unapologetic 'fearless freedom' for women and for all those who are oppressed and fearful today.

In 2012, we pointed out that the police, politicians, judges and campus administrators in India tended to understand sexual violence as a loss of 'honour' rather than as a violation of consent. This allows consensual inter-caste or interfaith relationships to be characterized as 'rape'. As a result, 'honour' crimes and patriarchal restrictions hide in plain sight, disguised as 'protecting women from rape'. This creates an upside-down reality, where consensual inter-caste and interfaith relationships are branded as 'rape'; assaults on women's autonomy are coded as 'safety'; and women's autonomy is used to label them 'dishonourable' and thus discredit rape complaints. This book, like the 2012 protests, tries to set reality the right side up.

Just as this book was ready to go into print in December 2019, something happened that forced me, and many of us, to revisit December 2012 and take stock of where we stand today, seven winters later, in India.

One night in late November 2019, a young veterinary doctor in Hyderabad called her sister from a toll station to say she had found a puncture in one of the tyres of her parked scooter.[1] She asked her sister to keep speaking to her, because she was wary of the men who had offered to help get the vehicle fixed. Soon after, her phone was found switched off, and her sister and parents, beside themselves with worry, headed out to the toll station. When they failed to find her, they went to the police, who laughed off their concerns, suggesting the woman must have eloped,[2] and wasted four precious hours before launching a search for her. The next morning, her charred body was found under a bridge.[3]

People erupted in protest not only in Telangana but all over India, in grief and rage, much as they had in December 2012 after the gang-rape of a woman on a Delhi bus. In 2019, as in 2012, substantial sections of angry people demanded that the accused be hanged. On both occasions, people were angry with the police's unwillingness to take complaints of violence against women seriously. On both occasions, many displayed impatience with the protracted processes of the legal system, and instead felt that the accused should simply be 'handed over to the public' to be lynched. In spite of the similarities, however, there are significant differences between the two incidents. If 2012 marks the moment that the feminist demand for 'fearless freedom' made itself heard over the din for the 'death penalty', 2019 is the moment that we see a concerted effort by power and its propagandists to discredit that demand.

The same Hyderabad police that had laughed off the concerns of the victim's sister and parents when they tried to get the police to find her and save her life issued an 'advisory'[4] for women in the wake of the rape-murder. The advisory was met with anger by women. They pointed out that they did not need the police to tell them what precautions to take—they 'take a million precautions anyway'. This victim in particular might have been alive and well had the police been patrolling the area where she was attacked, or if they had at least launched a search for her as soon as they were alerted by members of her family that she could be in trouble.

Yet again, women were being told they could avoid rape and violence if only they followed 'advice' given to them and restricted their access to public spaces. To women, however, it is crystal clear that what makes streets safer is not fewer but more women. Public spaces bustling with women immediately invite all women to feel less fear. A simple measure that would go a long way in implementing this is 24/7 public transport that is safe, affordable and regular as clockwork. If Priyanka in Hyderabad or Jyoti in Delhi could have been sure of getting a public bus, they would probably have been safe and well today. A public-transport infrastructure with last-mile connectivity promotes fearless freedom.

Instead of being held accountable for their failure to do what is in their power to make women more safe and welcome in public spaces, governments are finding it easier in 2019 to distract us with the mirage of the 'death penalty' and other 'solutions' that are as counterfeit as they are dangerous.

A Telangana minister, son of Chief Minister K. Chandrasekhar Rao, said he understood why people wanted to 'hang them (the four suspects) in public immediately or shoot them',[5] but that, unfortunately, the laws as they stand today do not allow this. He asked Prime Minister Narendra Modi to amend the law to ensure that those who rape women and children 'are given capital punishment without delay'.[6] In the Parliament, Rajya Sabha MP Jaya Bachchan called for the suspects in the Hyderabad case to be lynched in public.[7] Days later, the Hyderabad police shot dead the four unarmed rape-murder suspects in the dead of night, in what they claimed was self-defence. All over India, the custodial killing is widely believed to be an execution—and, ominously, is being welcomed and celebrated as 'justice'. There is a growing clamour for the Modi government to execute the convicts who are on death row in the 2012 rape-murder case.

Such 'solutions' do not make women safer—in fact, the opposite is true. In our discussion of Saudi Arabia in Chapter 6, we saw that laws that are in tune with popular patriarchal morality might prescribe cruel punishments for rapists, but are dangerous because they also define rape as 'dishonour' and punish the victims. Such laws fail to recognize or address the harm of rape and are, therefore, dangerous and detrimental to women.

If you look closely at the social media handles and television channels that celebrate lynching and custodial killing as 'justice' for victims who have been killed, you will most likely find that the same Twitter handles and TV channels also accuse victims who are alive and seeking justice of 'misusing' rape, sexual harassment and domestic-violence laws. They are also likely to profile feminists and women students who demand autonomy as 'anti-nationals' (left-wing extremists) or proponents of 'free sex'. Check out the Twitter handles and TV channels that attack the merest suggestion that the guilt of the Hyderabad rape suspects executed by the police was not proven. Did they also run conspiracy theories proclaiming the innocence of the men convicted in the Kathua rape and murder case?

Republic TV, which regularly attacks feminist activists, including me, as 'anti-national',[8] ran hashtags such as #DeathForRapists on the Hyderabad rape-murder,[9] and #HyderabadJustice celebrating the fake encounter.[10] When you see such coverage, it is a good time to remember Meena Khalko and Thangjam Manorama, whose stories you have read in the final chapter of this book. Meena and Manorama were gang-raped and killed by the Chhattisgarh police and Assam Rifles personnel, respectively. Their murders were dressed up as 'encounters', and despite judicial commissions nailing the lies, their rapists and killers have so far avoided even having to face trial. A police force that can kill with impunity, no questions asked, can also gang-rape and kill women with impunity, confident that no questions will be asked. It is also important to remember what Republic TV did to Sudha Bharadwaj, the courageous lawyer who helped Meena Khalko's parents seek justice.[11] In July 2018, Republic TV used a concocted letter to profile Sudha Bharadwaj as an 'urban Naxal', following which she was arrested by the Pune police.[12] For the past year, this sterling feminist activist and human rights lawyer has been in jail, while the police have failed to provide an iota of evidence for her involvement in any crime.[13]

In 2012, feminists could call out the bad faith of governments and politicians in calling for the death penalty instead of answering for their failures—and still be heard and understood. We managed to shift the discourse in the anti-rape movement away from knee-jerk cries for revenge in one particular case towards an uncompromising demand for 'fearless freedom' for women, for sexual and gender minorities—and for everyone else. We could stand among thousands of angry protesters in Delhi, and persuade them to give up 'hang/lynch the rapist' slogans in favour of 'women want freedom' slogans, without risking violence or abuse.[14] Demanding accountability and an end to impunity, we could make ourselves heard above the 'death penalty' din. We could criticize the prime minister and the ruling party without being deluged by rape threats and death threats. Not so this time.

In an essay in 2013, in which she referred to the anti-rape movement in India that year, American writer Rebecca Solnit observed:

There is . . . a pattern of violence against women that's broad and deep and horrific and incessantly overlooked.

Occasionally, a case involving a celebrity or lurid details in a particular case get a lot of attention in the media, but such cases are treated as anomalies, while the abundance of incidental news items about violence against women in this country, in other countries, on every continent including Antarctica, constitute a kind of background wallpaper for the news . . . We have dots so close they're splatters melting into a stain, but hardly anyone connects them, or names that stain. In India they did. They said that this is a civil rights issue, it's a human rights issue, it's everyone's problem, it's not isolated, and it's never going to be acceptable again. It has to change. It's your job to change it, and mine, and ours.[15]

This time, Indian feminists have been besieged by armies of trolls every day, who take their cue from ruling-party politicians and prime-time anchors to label us 'anti-national' for daring to assert that feminist and human rights principles are not only compatible but inseparable. The patriarchal propagandists are determined this time to make us believe that instances such as the Hyderabad rape-murder are anomalies that can be avenged by hanging or custodial killing—and that it is feminists and human rights activists who stand in the way of justice. In the face of this organized hostility, feminist movements in India keep working, patiently, to connect the dots between gender-based violence by random strangers; domestic violence and violence against women's autonomy in households, hostels and factories; custodial violence by the armed forces in conflict areas; and various counterfeit 'solutions' for gender-based violence that are actually making the problem worse.

Women's movements in India do not want a mythical 'collective conscience' appeased by the summary execution of men whom the police declares rapists. Instead, we want society's conscience to change and become more respectful of consent and of women's autonomy. Because the patriarchal propagandists are trying to drown out our voices, you, the concerned Indian, have to work harder to be able to hear what feminists are saying. You may not get to hear us at all on television. Most television propagandists and powerful politicians would have you believe they are the true anti-rape crusaders while feminists are the villains.

I hope and trust, however, that many of you who strive for real understanding rather than a temporary dopamine hit will reach out for this book, read it, share it and recommend it to your friends. This book is not the end of a journey—it is an invitation to join feminists in hoping and working towards a better India and a better world.

NOTES

Introduction: If You Want to Be Safe, Why Do You Demand Freedom?

1. Tarique Anwar, 'Girl Students Invite Trouble By Stepping Out of Hostels After 8 PM, Says BHU VC', NewsClick, 28 September 2017.

Chapter 1: Raksha Bandhan: Loving Bondage

1. John Berger, *Ways of Seeing* (London: Penguin Books, 1972), p. 46.
2. 'Women don't get raped if parked at home like cars: Andhra Assembly speaker', The News Minute, 10 February 2017.
3. Mohammed Iqbal, 'Married women safer on streets: HC', *The Hindu*, September 30, 2014
4. 'Global and regional estimates of violence against women: Prevalence and health effects of intimate partner violence and non-partner sexual violence', World Health Organization, Department of Reproductive Health and Research, London School of Hygiene and Tropical Medicine, South African Medical Research Council.

5. *'Behind Closed Doors: 20 years of the Women's Aid Femicide Monitoring Project, 1996-2016'*, Women's Aid, Ireland, November 2016.

6. Gorakh Pandey, 'Band Khidkiyon Se Takrakar', http://mrityubodh.blogspot.com/2011/01/blog-post_29.html, accessed 18 September 2019.

7. L. Subaiya and R. Vanneman, 'The Multi-dimensionality of Development and Gender Empowerment: Women's Decision-Making and Mobility in India', draft, India Human Development Survey, 29 September 2016.

8. Rukmini S., 'The many shades of rape cases in Delhi', *The Hindu*, 29 July 2014.

9. Ibid.

10. Ibid.

11. Rukmini S., 'Young love often reported as rape in our "cruel society"', *The Hindu*, 31 July 2014.

12. '"Unnatural Offences": Obstacles to Justice in India Based on Sexual Orientation and Gender Identity', International Commission of Jurists, February 2017, pp. 48–49.

13. Ibid.

14. Ibid.

15. Uma Chakravarti, *Gendering Caste: Through a Feminist Lens* (Calcutta: Stree, 2003), pp. 35–36.

16. Ibid, pp. 152–53.

17. Prem Chowdhry, Contentious Marriages, *Eloping Couples: Gender, Caste, and Patriarchy in Northern India* (New Delhi: Oxford University Press, 2007).

18. Alok Dhanwa, 'Bhagi Hui Ladkiyan', भागी_हुई_लड़कियां_/_आलोक_धन्वा, http://kavitakosh.org/kk/भागी_हुई_लड़कियां_/_आलोक_धन्वा, accessed 7 September 2019, translation by Kavita Krishnan.

19. 'When the world is upside down, it is the portent of destruction . . . The serfs will say, "Hey you!", the Brahmins will say, "Pray, sir!" . . .'

Brahmins, barons and commoners will mix marriages and become like serfs, without austerity or truth . . . The women are corrupt and, secretly deceiving their husbands, lasciviously fornicate with slaves and cattle. No father will condone his son, no son his father, and not a wife will be obedient to her husband . . . This world will be totally upside down . . . The serfs will refuse to serve the twice-born . . .', *The Mahabharata, Volume 2: The Book of the Assembly Hall, The Book of the Forest*, translated and edited by J.A.B. Buitenen, (Chicago: University of Chicago Press, 1975), pp. 586–598.

20. Arti Dhand, *Woman as Fire, Woman as Sage: Sexual Ideology in the Mahabharata* (State University of New York Press, 2008), p. 119.

21. Ibid, p. 120.

22. Ibid, pp. 122–23.

23. *The Bhagavad Gita*, Twenty-Fifth-Anniversary Edition, translated by Winthrop Sargeant, edited and with a preface by Christopher Key Chapple (State University of New York Press, 2009), pp. 79–81.

24. Tweet dated 2 January 2018, https://twitter.com/abhijitmajumder/status/948217152800137216?s=19, accessed 1 January 2019.

25. Tweet dated 3 January 2018, https://twitter.com/abhijitmajumder/status/948448968945512448, accessed on 1 January 2019.

26. *The Bhagavad Gita*, Twenty-Fifth-Anniversary Edition, translated by Winthrop Sargeant, edited and with a preface by Christopher Key Chapple (State University of New York Press, 2009), p. 192.

27. Ibid, p. 213.

28. Ibid, pp. 708–09. The translator specifies here that where the text refers to 'one's own duty' and the 'duty of another', 'caste duty is meant'.

29. Ibid, pp. 702–705.

30. Arti Dhand, *Woman as Fire, Woman as Sage: Sexual Ideology in the Mahabharata* (State University of New York Press, 2008), p. 148.
31. Ibid, pp. 184–85.
32. 'Documentary: Why Do Haryana's Old and Young Blame Women for Rape?', The Quint, 1 May 2019.
33. Girija Borker, 'Safety First: Perceived Risk of Street Harassment and Educational Choices of Women', Job Market Paper, 3 November 2017, https://girijaborker.files.wordpress.com/2017/11/borker_jmp.pdf, accessed 26 November 2019.
34. Jitender Chattar, '"I vowed to punish my wife's rapists," says husband of rape survivor', Hindustan Times, 14 January 2019.

Chapter 2: Organized Crimes against Women's Freedom

1. Shakti Vahini vs Union of India, 27 March 2018.
2. 'Dashing hopes, Emboldening khaps—the High Court verdict on the Manoj Babli case', NewsClick, 18 March 2011.
3. Ibid.
4. S. Anand, 'Mirchpur: A Dog Story', *Open*, 1 May 2010.
5. J. Venkatesan, 'SC notice to Haryana over Dalit families flight from Mirchpur', *The Hindu*, 31 May 2010.
6. 'SC Directs Magisterial Probe into Mirchpur Dalit Case', The *Indian Express*, 5 April 2011.
7. Pragati Ratti, 'Freedom must have limits too, girls should dress decently to not lure boys, says BJP's Karnal candidate', News18, 10 October 2014.
8. 'Hooda defends Khaps, says they don't order honour killings', *Business Standard*, 5 October 2013.
9. Rajesh Ahuja, 'Most people happy with functioning of khaps: Hooda', *The Hindu*, 9 November 2016.
10. Vishal Joshi and Aurangzeb Naqshbandi, 'Naveen Jindal, Chautala join hands, lobby for khap panchayats', *Hindustan Times*, 11 May 2010.

11. Arvind Kejriwal, *Swaraj* (Noida: HarperCollins India, 2012), p. 46.

12. Yogendra Yadav, Facebook post dated 31 January 2014, https://www.facebook.com/YogendraYY/posts/601060556629023?__xts__[0]=68.ARAzf TPLgacvJdWu73zIZM0XrdGdj7-NUCC-o9GDC 36KowtwedbDkzkVJOWQ_USiHflGd-0pG WYzlPGVvTCPONGk0aZD3dmCTnXUuu-nz7-8zq1e Bx9PaTKv0cjIA5f4q5uQ3wwB6TKSWHoiqIAKr2jbelZ, accessed 8 June 2019.

13. Gargi Parsai, 'Khap panchayats have no legal sanctity, says Yogendra Yadav', *The Hindu*, 2 February 2014.

14. 'An Interview with Jagmati Sangwan', *Sanhati*, 17 April 2017.

15. Amit Thorat and Diane Coffey, 'Still frowning upon intermarriages,' *The Hindu*, 3 January 2017.

16. B. Kolappan, 'Ramadoss consolidates intermediate caste groups against Dalits', *The Hindu*, 18 October 2016.

17. '"After falling in love, I saw the reality of caste": E. Ilavarasan', interview with writer Kavin Malar in the Tamil edition of the *India Today* magazine, translated by Prakash Venkatesan, *Kafila*, 5 July 2013.

18. Sowmya Sivakumar, 'Ilavarasan's Death Was Definitely "Not a Suicide", Says Doctor Who Examined Body', The Wire, 15 March 2017.

19. Ilangovan Rajasekaran, 'He should have realized his birth-based limitations', *Frontline*, 7 August 2015, Volume 32, Issue 15.

20. 'KJK merges with BJP, G.K. Nagaraj joins party', *The Hindu*, 5 September 2017.

21. Tweet by S. Gurumurthy dated 7 August 2014, https://twitter.com/sgurumurthy/status/497625183809593344, accessed 4 January 2019.

22. See Shilpa Phadke, Sameera Khan and Shilpa Ranade, *Why Loiter? Women & Risk on Mumbai Streets* (New Delhi: Penguin Books India, 2011), and Mini Dixit, 'A simultaneous protest

in seven cities against hostel rules imposed after December 16, was highly inspiring', *India Today*, 17 December 2015.

23. *Puthumai Penn*, Subramania Bharati, *Bharathiar Kavithaigal*, People's Edition (Chennai: Kavitha Publications, 2006). Translated from Tamil by Kavita Krishnan.

24. Ibid.

25. Dionne Bunsha, 'A serial kidnapper and his "mission"', *Frontline*, Volume 23, Issue 25, 16–29 December 2006.

26. 'The Truth: Gujarat 2002: Babu Bajrangi', TehelkaTV, posted on YouTube, 25 October 2007, https://www.youtube.com/watch?v=mfnTl_Fwvbo, accessed 8 June 2019.

27. 'Naroda Patiya riots: BJP MLA Maya Kodnani sentenced to 28 years in jail, Babu Bajrangi life', *The Indian Express*, 31 August 2012.

28. 'Supreme Court Grants Bail to Babu Bajrangi', *The Hindu*, 7 March 2019.

29. 'Operation Juliet: Busting the Bogey of "Love Jihad"', Cobrapost, 4 October 2015, https://www.cobrapost.com/blog/operation-juliet-busting-the-bogey-of-love-jihad-2/900, accessed 8 June 2019.

30. Ibid.

31. Ibid.

32. Ibid.

33. 'BJP Leader, Activists Disrupt Hindu–Muslim Wedding Celebration in Ghaziabad', The Wire, 23 December 2017.

34. Harsh Mander, 'With his multi-faith iftar in Delhi, Ankit Saxena's father sets an example for these fraught times', Scroll.in, 7 June 2018.

Chapter 3: Profiles in Courage

1.   Neha Dixit, 'Exposing Love Jehad', NewsClick, 18 October 2014. A longer version of this story originally appeared in www.aljazeera.com.

2. Harper Lee, *To Kill a Mockingbird* (Philadelphia: J.B. Lippincott & Co., 1960).

3. Sourodipto Sanyal, 'Love Jihad in 2014, staid silence now: Zee News' narrative around the Meerut "gang rape"', Newslaundry, 16 December 2015.

4. For example, see a tweet dated 17 August 2017 by Times Now, airing a clip from a Times Now show, claiming 'Kerala's love jihad victim Athira in a stunning confession, claims that hate preachings were used to brainwash girls #HinduGirlsForISIS', https://twitter.com/TimesNow/status/898223950978789376?s=19, accessed 8 November 2019. Also see 'Kerala "love jihad" case: 105 women converted in last one year', YouTube, airing a Times Now story, 31 August 2017, https://www.youtube.com/watch?v=BmP8-Gnpw8w, accessed 8 November 2019.

5. Anusha Soni, 'How Supreme Court failed by delaying to restore Hadiya's marriage', DailyO, 9 March 2018.

6. 'SC "Allows" Hadiya, an Adult Woman, to Go to Tamil Nadu for Studies', The Wire, 27 November 2017.

7. Megha Varier, 'Hadiya's Case: What Happened in Court Hall No. 1 of the Supreme Court', The News Minute, 28 November 2017.

8. Ibid.

9. *Puthumai Penn*, Subramania Bharati, *Bharathiar Kavithaigal*, People's Edition (Chennai: Kavitha Publications, 2006). Translated from Tamil by Kavita Krishnan.

10. Gopika Ajayan and Megha Varier, 'New tangles in Hadiya row: "Yoga centre" members tortured me to re-convert, she reveals', The News Minute, 29 November 2017.

11. Megha Varier, 'Tortured for 22 days: Hindu woman married to Christian exposes Kerala's "anti-conversion clinic"', The News Minute, 26 September 2017.

12. 'Court Can't Decide Marriage Is Invalid, Hadiya Can Choose Independently, Says SC Judge', The Wire, 23 January 2018.

13. Kathir Vincent, 'They Killed My Husband, Saying, "How Dare You Love, You Pallar Son-of-a-Bitch?"', HuffPost, 15 July 2016.

14. National Family Health Survey 2015–16 (NFHS-4) found that just 41 per cent of Indian women aged between fifteen and forty-nine are allowed to go alone to the market, to the health centre and outside the community (NFHS-4, Table 15.13).

15. Kathir Vincent, 'They Killed My Husband, Saying, "How Dare You Love, You Pallar Son-of-a-Bitch?"', HuffPost, 15 July 2016.

16. Ibid.

17. Priyanka Thirumurthy, 'Living to defy caste: Kausalya's incredible journey since her husband was hacked for "honour"', The News Minute, 15 March 2017.

18. Mayilvaganan, 'How a young widow brought her father to book', The Times of India, 26 December 2017.

19. Kathir Vincent, 'They Killed My Husband, Saying, "How Dare You Love, You Pallar Son-of-a-Bitch?"', HuffPost, 15 July 2016. 2016.

20. Ibid.

21. Ibid.

22. Ibid.

23. Ibid.

24. Ibid.

25. Dhrubo Jyoti, 'India at 70 | "I'm not Afraid": Husband murdered, Kausalya fights honour killings', Hindustan Times, 13 August 2017.

26. Kavitha Muralidharan, 'When Kausalya met Divya: Coming together of 2 women who remind us of the ugliness of caste', The News Minute, 15 April 2017.

27. P.V. Srividya, 'TN circular sneaks in parental consent in marriage registration', The Hindu, 11 March 2018.

28. Prerna Gauba, 'I can't believe that Nitish chose someone so weak like Bharti Yadav: Nilam Katara', Hindustan Times, 17 May 2018.

Chapter 4: 'Empowering' Women?

1. Kalpana Sharma, 'Maneka Gandhi's suggestion on mandatory sex tests aims to absolve doctors of blame for foeticide', Scroll.in, 4 February 2016.
2. Margaret Atwood's novels *The Handmaid's Tale* and *The Testaments* are set in such a dystopia.
3. Priyanka Kotamraju, 'No bibi in Bibipur', *The Hindu BusinessLine*, 12 September 2014.
4. Ibid.
5. 'BJP leader promises brides from Bihar for Haryana youths', *The Indian Express*, 7 July 2014.
6. Kumkum Sangari, *Solid: Liquid: A (Trans)national Reproductive Formation* (New Delhi: Tulika Books, 2015).
7. Priyanka Bhattacharya, 'Why "Swachh India" Is the Biggest Women's Movement at the Moment', NDTV, 3 March 2017.
8. '#EveryWomansRight—An Initiative By Astral Pipes', YouTube, 21 May 2017, https://www.youtube.com/watch?v=QXCOUQ7ZBko, accessed 9 June 2019.
9. Nikhil Srivastav and Aashish Gupta, 'Why Using Patriarchal Messaging to Promote Toilets Is a Bad Idea', *The Wire*, 7 June 2015
10. https://twitter.com/swachhbharat/status/869437001329782784?lang=gl, image tweeted from @ swacchbharat handle, accessed 8 November 2019.
11. 'UNICEF Total Sanitation TVC 3 DULHAN Featuring Vidya Balan', YouTube, 6 May 2013, https://www.youtube.com/watch?v=oBKeZmJeoy4, accessed 8 November 2019
12. http://www.communityledtotalsanitation.org/sites/communityledtotalsanitation.org/files/MP_NBA_MARYADA_guidelines.pdf, accessed 9 June 2019.
13. Poster in possession of the writer, accessed through activists in Bihar.

14. Vyas Mohan, 'Rajasthan Wants Teachers to Make Early Morning Rounds, Click Pics to Check Open Defecation', HuffPost, 15 July 2016.

15. Angshuman Choudhury and Prannv Dhawan, 'Impunity for cow vigilantes in BJP's India threatens the foundational idea of the country's pluralism', Firstpost, April 13 2019.

16. Shruti Jain, 'Dirty Backstory to "Swachch Bharat" Lynching: No Toilets, No Water and the Threat of Eviction', The Wire, 22 June 2017.

17. Salil Mekaad, 'Villager forced to clean his feces with hands in Ujjain as part of Swachh Bharat Abhiyan', The Times of India, 29 December 2016.

18. Rashmi Drolia, 'Man killed for buying time to build toilet', The Times of India, 8 October 2016.

19. 'Bihar: Children Jump into Pond, Saved as Officials Chase Villagers Defecating In Open', The *Bihar Post*, 3 August 2017.

20. Liz Chatterjee, 'Time to acknowledge the dirty truth behind community-led sanitation', The *Guardian*, 9 June 2011.

21. Achyut Mishra, '"Nudge" is the secret behind success of Modi's pet projects, says Economic Survey', *The Print*, 4 July 2019.

22. ET Online, 'Modi government had already put Nobel winner's idea into practice', The Economic Times, 10 October 2017.

23. Suchitra Vijayan and Arjun Singh Sethi, 'The Gates Foundation shouldn't give an award to Narendra Modi', The *Washington Post*, 7 September 2019.

24. Diane Coffey, Aashish Gupta, Payal Hathi, Dean Spears, Nikhil Srivastav and Sangita Vyas, 'Untouchability, Pollution, and Latrine Pits: Understanding Open Defecation in Rural India', *Economic and Political Weekly*, Volume 52, Issue 1, 7 January 2017.

25. Ibid.

26. Shilpa Phadke, Sameera Khan and Shilpa Ranade, *Why Loiter? Women and Risk on Mumbai Streets* (New Delhi: Penguin Books India, 2011).

27. Shilpa Phadke, 'Better Toilets Won't Solve India's Rape Problem: Women Need to Feel Safe in Public, Not Hide in Private', Al Jazeera, 17 June 2014.

28. Diane Coffey, Aashish Gupta, Payal Hathi, Dean Spears, Nikhil Srivastav, Sangita Vyas, 'Untouchability, Pollution, and Latrine Pits: Understanding Open Defecation in Rural India', *Economic and Political Weekly*, volume 52, issue 1, 7 January 2017.

29. Rukmini S., 'Just 5% of Indian marriages are inter-caste: survey', The Hindu, 13 November 2014.

30. English rendering of Prime Minister Shri Narendra Modi's address to the nation from the ramparts of the Red Fort on the 73rd Independence Day—15 August 2019, released by the Prime Minister's Office, https://www.pib.nic.in/PressReleasePage.aspx?PRID=1582107, last accessed 14 September 2019.

31. Kavita Krishnan, 'Chhattisgarh's Sterilization Horror: Kavita Krishnan on "Women as Wombs"', Youth Ki Awaaz, 17 November 2014.

32. Soutik Biswas, 'India's dark history of sterilisation', BBC, 14 November 2014.

33. The proceedings of this public hearing are described in detail by the author here: Kavita Krishnan, 'Mother's Day 2016: What the State Owes Mothers, Parents and Women', *SabrangIndia*, 8 May 2016, https://sabrangindia.in/article/mothers-day-2016-what-state-owes-mothers-parents-and-women; https://protect-eu.mimecast.com/s/ntlmCP7jETNz1mVIjq0jM?domain=sabrang.in.

34. 'Should We Run Relief Camps? Open Child Producing Centres?', excerpts from a translation of an audio recording

of Narendra Modi's speech at Becharaji, Gujarat, on 9 September 2002 during his Gujarat Gaurav Yatra, *Outlook, 30 September 2002*, https://www.outlookindia.com/website/story/should-we-run-relief-camps-open-child-producing-centres/217398, accessed 14 September 2019.

35. 'MP Giriraj Singh blames Muslims as he calls for a law to control population', posted by *The Print*, YouTube, 14 July 2019, https://www.youtube.com/watch?v=UnGuY2eFQr8&t=122s, accessed 14 September 2019.

36. 'Operation Juliet: Busting the Bogey of "Love Jihad"', Cobrapost, 4 October 2015, https://www.cobrapost.com/blog/operation-juliet-busting-the-bogey-of-love-jihad-2/900, accessed 8 June 2019.

37. Kalpana Wilson, 'Towards a Radical Re-appropriation: Gender, Development and Neoliberal Feminism', *Development and Change*, 2015.

38. Ibid.

39. AP, 'Hundreds of Suicides in India Linked to Microfinance Organizations', Business Insider, 24 February 2012.

40. Jinka Nagaraju, 'MFI agents "forcing" debtors to commit suicide: Study', *The Times of India*, 20 October 2010.

41. 'Young Indians who make a difference', Rediff News, 27 March 2008.

42. Greg Chen, Stephen Rasmussen, Xavier Reille and Daniel Rozas, 'Indian Microfinance Goes Public: The SKS Initial Public Offering', Focus Note 65, Washington, DC: CGAP (Consultative Group to Assist the Poor), 2010.

43. Vikram Akula, *A Fistful of Rice: My Unexpected Quest to End Poverty through Profitability* (Harvard Business Review Press, 2010).

44. Ibid, p. 76.

45. Ibid, p. 82.

46. Chander Suta Dogra, 'Why Microfinance is Becoming a Bad Word All Over Again', The Wire, 15 January 2016.
47. Sathish G.T., 'Women Struggle to Repay Loans Taken from Microfinance Institutions', *The Hindu*, 18 December 2016.https://www.thehindu.com/todays-paper/tp-national/tp-karnataka/Women-struggle-to-repay-loans-taken-from-microfinance-institutions/article16898313.ece
48. 'Women allege coercive loan recovery by microfinance firms', *The Hindu*, 6 January 2017.
49. Moin Qazi, 'Why Microfinance Is an Ugly Word in India's Villages', DailyO, 16 December 2016.
50. 'Microfinance has failed in India: Jairam Ramesh', *Hindustan Times*, 6 December 2013.
51. Jaya Sharma, Soma K. Parthasarathy and Archana Dwivedi, 'Examining Self Help Groups: Empowerment, Poverty Alleviation, Education—A Quantitative Study', Nirantar, New Delhi, 2007.
52. Ibid.
53. Ibid.
54. Ibid.
55. Ibid.
56. Ibid.
57. Ibid.
58. Ibid.

Chapter 5: Factories as 'Families'

1. Nita Bhalla, 'Victoria's Secret bras a boost for rural indian women', Reuters, 22 May 2012.
2. Ibid.
3. Ibid.
4. 'Understanding the Characteristics of the Sumangali Scheme in Tamil Nadu Textile & Garment Industry and

Supply Chain Linkages', Solidaridad-South and South East Asia Report, 2012, https://www.fairlabor.org/blog/entry/understanding-sumangali-scheme-tamil-nadus-garment-textile-industry, accessed 20 December 2019.

5. Charukesi Ramadurai, 'Stitching Lingerie Improves Women's Lives in South India', The *New York Times*, 21 May 2012; Sadie Whitelocks, 'How Victoria's Secret Bras are Proving a Boost for the Indian Women Who Make Them', *Daily Mail*, 25 May 2012; Venkataraghavan Srinivasan, 'Victoria's Secret—"Made in Kanchipuram"', Linkedin.com, 4 April 2016.

6. 'Flawed Fabrics—The Abuse of Girls and Women Workers in the South Indian Textile Industry', a report by the Centre for Research on Multinational Corporations (SOMO) and the India Committee of the Netherlands (ICN), 2014.

7. Ibid, p. 6.

8. Ibid, p. 58.

9. Ibid, p. 52.

10. 'Production of Torture: A Study on Working Conditions Including Work-Place Harassments Facing Women Garment Workers in Bangalore and Other Districts', People's Union for Civil Liberties (PUCL) Karnataka, NLSIU, Bangalore, Vimochana, Alternative Law Forum (ALF), Concern-IISC, Manthan Law and Garments Mahila Karmikara Munnade, July 2016.

11. Ibid.

12. Ibid.

13. 'Flawed Fabrics—The Abuse of Girls and Women Workers in the South Indian Textile Industry', a report by the Centre for Research on Multinational Corporations (SOMO) and the India Committee of the Netherlands (ICN), 2014, p. 59.

14. Ibid, p. 57.

15. Ibid, p. 53.

16. 'Production of Torture: A Study on Working Conditions Including Work-Place Harassments Facing Women Garment Workers in Bangalore and Other Districts', People's Union for Civil Liberties (PUCL) Karnataka, NLSIU, Bangalore, Vimochana, Alternative Law Forum (ALF), Concern-IISC, Manthan Law and Garments Mahila Karmikara Munnade, July 2016.

17. Ibid.

18. Ibid.

19. Ibid.

20. 'Social reproduction' is a Marxist feminist term referring to the reproduction of labour power, of the next generation of workers and of social relationships. It refers to the perpetuation of society as we know it. Cooking, cleaning, care work, transport, schooling, healthcare—all are essential to making sure workers can replenish their exhausted labour power at the end of a day, and arrive refreshed at work again the next day. They are also essential to reproducing the next generation of workers. The bulk of this work is performed by unpaid or ill-paid women, often of oppressed races and castes.

21. Ibid.

22. Ibid.

23. 'Flawed Fabrics—The Abuse of Girls and Women Workers in the South Indian Textile Industry', a report by the Centre for Research on Multinational Corporations (SOMO) and the India Committee of the Netherlands (ICN), 2014, p. 70.

24. Ibid, pp. 53–54.

25. Ibid, pp. 6–7

26. Melissa Wright, *Disposable Women and Other Myths of Global Capitalism* (London and New York: Routledge, 2006).

27. Ibid.

28. Ibid, pp. 33–34.

29. Ibid.

30. Dina M. Siddiqi, 'Do Bangladeshi Factory Workers Need Saving? Sisterhood in the Post-Sweatshop Era', *Feminist Review*, Volume 91, 2009, pp. 154–174.

31. Lourdes Pantaleón and Fundación Laboral Dominicana 'Sexual Harassment in the Export Processing Zones of the Dominican Republic', International Labor Rights Fund, Rights for Working Women Campaign, May 2003.

32. Jayati Ghosh, *Never Done and Poorly Paid: Women's Work in Globalising India*, Women Unlimited, 2009, p. 123.

33. Ibid, p. 97.

34. http://tnlabour.in/wp-content/uploads/2015/04/The-Maruti-Struggle.pdf, accessed 9 June 2019.

35. 'India needs to be a low-cost hub for Make in India success: FM Arun Jaitley', *Business Today*, 30 January 2016.

36. 'Operation Juliet: Busting the Bogey of "Love Jihad"', Cobrapost, 4 October 2015, https://www.cobrapost.com/blog/operation-juliet-busting-the-bogey-of-love-jihad-2/900, accessed 8 June 2019.

37. Ibid.

38. Neha Dixit, 'Holier Than Cow', *Outlook*, 28 January 2013.

39. Kalpana Wilson, 'Agency as "Smart Economics": Neoliberalism, Gender and Development', in *Gender, Agency, and Coercion (Thinking Gender in Transnational Times Series)*, ed. Sumi Madhok, Anne Phillips and Kalpana Wilson (London: Palgrave Macmillan, 2013).

Chapter 6: Constructing a Fascist Patriarchy

1. Kumkum Sangari, 'The "Amenities of Domestic Life": Questions on Labour', *Social Scientist*, Volume 21, Number 9/11, September–October 1993, pp. 3–46.

2. Pratiksha Baxi, 'Netaji, unreformed', *The Indian Express*, 26 August 2015.

3. Kavita Krishnan, 'Patriarchal Ideology and Political Culture', Countercurrents.org, 25 May 2011.

4. Shreyasi Bose, 'A Culture of Victim Blaming: Suzette Jordan and Surviving Rape', Feminism In India, 28 November 2015.

5. '"Don't kill us, we want to live together": Kerala couple faces death threats', The News Minute, 20 July 2018.

6. Adolf Hitler, *Mein Kampf*, translated by Ralph Manheim (Boston: Houghton Mifflin Company, 1998), p. 253.

7. Max Doramus, *The Complete Hitler: A Digital Desktop Reference to His Speeches and Proclamations, 1932–45* (Bolchazy-Carducci Publishers, 1990), p. 532.

8. Neha Dixit, 'Holier Than Cow', *Outlook*, 28 January 2013.

9. James Q. Whitman, *Hitler's American Model, The United States and the Making of Nazi Race Law*, Princeton University Press, 2017.

10. 'Lynching in America: Confronting the Legacy of Racial Terror', Equal Justice Initiative, Third Edition, 2017.

11. Ida B. Wells, 'Lynching Our National Crime', Proceedings of the National Negro Conference, New York, 31 May 31 and 1 June, 1909, pp. 174–79, http://moses.law.umn.edu/darrow/documents/Proceedings%20of%20the%20National%20Negro%20Conference%201909_%20New%20York_%20May%2031%20and%20June_1.pdf, accessed 7 September 2019.

12. M.S. Golwalkar, *We or Our Nationhood Defined*, (Nagpur: Bharat Publications, 1939), pp. 47–48.

13. Ibid, p. 78.

14. Tom Treanor, *One Damn Thing After Another: The Adventures of an Innocent Man Trapped between Public Relations and the Axis* (New York: Doubleday, Doran & Company, Inc., 1944), p. 84.

15. 'WATCH: Sikh cop saves Muslim man from mob attack in Uttarakhand', *India Today*, 25 May 2018.

16. Video on Twitter, https://twitter.com/IronyOfIndia_/status/999716994772434944, accessed 17 January 2019.

17. 'BJP Leader Slaps Woman for Relationship with Muslim Man, Police Books Boyfriend', The Wire, 21 September 2017.

18. '"Hindu Ke Hote Huye Muslim Chahiye?" UP Police Beat Woman for Having Muslim Friend', posted by the Logical Indian, YouTube, https://www.youtube.com/watch?v=LbyNgbj7-Tw, accessed 9 June 2018.

19. 'Week After Meerut Assault Video, Rogue Cops Get "VIP" Transfer, No Arrest', NDTV, 1 October 2018.

20. 'Amit Shah's hate speech in Bijnor', YouTube, 4 April 2014, https://www.youtube.com/watch?v=PCjYDbwdQsY&t=40s, accessed 17 January 2019;

    Also see Mukul Kesavan's 'His Master's Voice—Amit Shah's Speeches in UP Belie the Promise of a New BJP', The Telegraph, 10 April 2014.

21. 'Amit Shah's Hate Speech at Jat Sabha in Shamli, West U.P.', posted by NewsClick, YouTube, 7 April 2014, https://www.youtube.com/watch?v=tTk_ZYdevoM, accessed 17 January 2019.

22. Manish Sahu, 'MoS Sanjeev Balyan visits Muzaffarnagar prison, meets 2013 riot accused', The Indian Express, 8 December 2015.

23. 'Operation Juliet: Busting the Bogey of "Love Jihad"', Cobrapost, 4 October 2015, https://www.cobrapost.com/blog/operation-juliet-busting-the-bogey-of-love-jihad-2/900, accessed 8 June 2019.

24. 'BJP MLA Suggests That Child Marriage Will Help End 'Love Jihad'', Scroll.in, 6 May 2018.

25. Trevor Noah, Born a Crime: Stories from a South African Childhood (Spiegel and Grau, 2016).

26. Radhika Ramaseshan, 'Modi chants purification mantra', The Telegraph, 26 September 2016.

27. Deendayal Upadhyay, 'Akhand Bharat: Dhyey Our Sadhan', *Panchjanya*, 24 August 1953, available on deendayalupadhyay. org, accessed 9 June 2019, translated by author.

28. Interview with Narendra Modi, https://www.jansatta.com/ national/live-pm-narendra-modi-interview-on-network-18-ibn-7-ibn-lokmat-cnbc-tv-18-etv-network/138681/, Jansatta Online, 2 September 2016.

29. Narendra Modi, *Social Harmony*, edited by Kishor Makwana, translated into English by Devang Nanavati, translation edited by Dr Avani Desai, Dr Alpa Shah and Dr Radhika Nagrath (New Delhi: Prabhat Prakashan, 2015), available at http://www.narendramodi.in/ebooks/social-harmony

30. B.R. Ambedkar, *Annihilation of Caste: The Annotated Critical Edition*, Navayana, 2014.

31. Vasant Moon, ed., *Dr Babasaheb Ambedkar Writings and Speeches, Vol. 17*, Part 3, education department, Government of Maharashtra, 14 April 1994, pp. 282–83.

32. India's land ceiling laws, enacted as part of the bid to end *zamindari* (landlordism), fix the maximum permitted size of landholding that an individual/a family can own. Land over and above this ceiling is called 'ceiling surplus land', and can be acquired by the government and redistributed among the landless poor.

33. Kavita Krishnan, 'Public Secrets Now Proven: Ranveer Sena Terrorists Caught on Camera by Cobrapost', Kafila, 23 August 2015.

34. Giridhar Jha, 'Bihar minister sparks controversy by calling slain Ranvir Sena chief a "true Gandhian"', *India Today*, 8 June 2012.

35. Dan Morrison, 'A Final Interview with Brahmeshwar Nath Singh', The *New York Times*, 4 June 2012.

36. Ram Madhav, 'Coming Full Circle at 70', *The Indian Express*, 15 August 2017.

37. Neha Dixit, 'Holier Than Cow', Outlook, 28 January 2013.

38. Ibid.

39. Ibid.

40. Ibid.

41. Ibid.

42. Ibid.

43. *Women and the Hindu Right: A Collection of Essays*, Tanika Sarkar and Urvashi Butalia eds., Kali for Women, 1995, pp. 332–33.

44. Ram Madhav, 'Coming Full Circle at 70', The Indian Express, 15 August 2017.

45. Speech made by B.R. Ambedkar while moving the draft constitution in the constituent assembly, Vasant Moon ed., *Dr Babasaheb Ambedkar Writings and Speeches, Volume 13*, education department, Government of Maharashtra, 14 April 1994, p. 61.

46. Ibid, pp. 405-06.

47. Adhiraj Nayar, 'Why Jaitley Needs to Study the Link Between RSS and Fascism', NewsClick, 28 June 2018.

48. 'Narendra Modi on MS Golwalkar, translated by Aakar Patel - Part 1', The *Caravan*, 31 May 2014.

49. Anubhuti Vishnoi, 'Uttar Pradesh: Yogi Adityanath had opposed women quota, defied BJP line in Parliament', The *Economic Times*, 20 March 2017.

50. http://www.yogiadityanath.in/lekh/lekh_7793_22021405312122022014.pdf, accessed 9 June 2019.

51. Omar Rashid, 'Yogi Adityanath emerging as BJP's star campaigner', *The Hindu*, 8 December 2018.

52. Mais Haddad, 'Victims of Rape and Law: How the Arab world laws protect the rapist, not the victim', Jurist, 9 May 2017.

53. Aida Alami, 'A Loophole for Rapists Is Eliminated in Morocco', *The New York Times*, 23 January 2014.

54. Daniel Howden, 'In the name of God: the Saudi rape victim's tale', *The Independent*, 29 November 2007.

55. Katherine Zoepf, 'Saudi King Pardons Rape Victim Sentenced to Be Lashed, Saudi Paper Reports', *The New York Times*, 18 December 2007.

56. Jawaharlal Nehru on 5 January 1961, quoted in A.G. Noorani's 'Ayodhya and Advani', *Mainstream*, 13 October 1990, p. 8.

57. B.R. Ambedkar, *Pakistan or the Partition of India, Dr Babasaheb Ambedkar Writings and Speeches*, Volume 8, Vasant Moon ed., education department, Government of Maharashtra, 14 April 1994, reprinted by Dr Ambedkar Foundation, January 2014, p. 358.

58. 'Haryana govt faces backlash after ad describing "ghoonghat" as identity of the state appears in magazine', *The Indian Express*, 28 June 2017.

59. Pheroze L. Vincent, 'Ben vs Ben, "Ram" still silent', The *Telegraph*, 22 June 2018.

Chapter 7: Where Women Are Worshipped, Can Women Roam?

1. Arundhati Roy, *The God of Small Things* (Noida: Random House, 2008), p. 299.

2. Ibid, p. 63.

3. E.M.S. Namboodiripad, 'Arundhati Royyude saundaryadarshanam', *Deshabhimani*, 29 November 1997.

4. Tanika Sarkar, 'Reflections on Birati Rape Cases: Gender Ideology in Bengal', *Economic and Political Weekly*, Volume 26, Issue 5, 2 February 1991, pp. 215–218.

5. Ibid.

6. *Women Writing in India: 600 B.C. to the Present – Volume I: 600 B.C. to the Early 20th Century*, Susie Tharu and K. Lalita eds., (New York: The Feminist Press, 1991), p. 68.

7. Ibid.

8. Tanika Sarkar, *Hindu Wife, Hindu Nation: Community, Religion and Cultural Nationalism* (New Delhi: Orient Blackswan, 2003), p. 109.

9. Ibid, p. 121.

10. Tanika Sarkar, *Words to Win – The Making of Amar Jiban: A Modern Autobiography* (New Delhi: Kali for Women, 1999), p. 167.

11. Ibid.

12. Ibid, pp. 159–160.

13. Ibid, p. 168.

14. Tanika Sarkar, *Hindu Wife, Hindu Nation: Community, Religion and Cultural Nationalism* (New Delhi: Orient Blackswan, 2003), p. 129.

15. 'Rajasthan MLA Gyan Dev Ahuja says JNU produces 3,000 used condoms every day', *India Today*, 22 February 2016.

16. 'The Newshour Debate: Apology or Arrogance?—Full Debate', YouTube, posted by Times Now, 9 December 2013, https://www.youtube.com/watch?v=zgFrc5UNkFs, minutes 19:36 20:28. Also tweet by Subramanian Swamy, 'When I said Naxals believe in free sex I did not know Tejpal dictum: that modern secular girls will not object to sexual free enterprise', 18 January 2014, https://twitter.com/Swamy39/status/424755865023807488, accessed 9 June 2019. Also see Swamy's tweet dated 29 October 2015, replying to Kavita Krishnan's tweet calling out an airline for barring a woman in a short skirt from a flight, by saying, 'These free sex Naxalites will defend passengers on flight wearing bikinis to rubbish "middle class" values', https://newsable.asianetnews.com/karnataka/here-is-the-truth-behind-gauri-lankeshs-free-sex-comment-and-subramanian-swamy-is-to-be-blamed-for-it accessed 9 June 2019.

17. 'JNU is a den of organized sex racket, says dossier prepared by university teachers', *India Today*, 29 April 2016.

18. Tanika Sarkar, *Hindu Wife, Hindu Nation: Community, Religion and Cultural Nationalism* (New Delhi: Orient Blackswan, 2003), p. 129.

19. Bal Gangadhar Tilak, *Kesari*, 22 March 1887, translated by Parnal Chirmuley.

20. Bal Gangadhar Tilak, 'Our System of Education: A Defect and a Cure', *Mahratta*, 15 May 1881, pp. 3–4.

21. Ibid.

22. Bal Gangadhar Tilak, 'Letter to the editor by "an observer from within"', *Mahratta*, 5 May 1901, p. 9.

23. Bal Gangadhar Tilak, *Kesari*, 25 October 1887.

24. Bal Gangadhar Tilak, cited in *Educating the Nation: Documents on the Discourse of National Education in India 1880–1920*, S. Bhattacharya, J Bara and C.R Yagati eds., document number 109, pp. 211–212.

Chapter 8: Mothers and Motherlands

1. 'Letter Number 314', *Selected Letters of Rabindranath Tagore*, K. Datta and A. Robinson eds., Cambridge University Press, 1997.

2. On 14 August 1947, just on the eve of India's Independence, the RSS organ *Organiser* declared, 'The people who have come to power by the kick of fate may give in our hands the Tricolour but it will never be respected and owned by Hindus. The word three is in itself an evil and a flag having three colours will certainly produce a very bad psychological effect and is injurious to a country.'

3. '"Vande Mataram" is real national anthem: RSS', *Deccan Herald*, 3 April 2016. In RSS shakhas, it is the saffron flag and the unedited 'Vande Mataram' that are prescribed; never the 'Jana Gana Mana' and the tricolour.

4. Tanika Sarkar, *Hindu Wife, Hindu Nation: Community, Religion and Cultural Nationalism* (New Delhi: Orient Blackswan, 2003), p. 273.

5. Sanjay Kumar Jha, 'Laloo Prasad Yadav finds himself under fire from students', India Today, 15 May 1997.

6. Kavita Krishnan, 'Radhika Vemula lost her son. Now she's being insulted by the Modi government', Scroll.in, 31 January 2016.

7. Abhishek Dey, 'A year after JNU student Najeeb Ahmad went missing, his mother continues to wait for answers', Scroll.in, 15 October 2017.

8. Deepender Deswal, 'Manoj's mother, sister fear threat to life', The Times of India, 14 March 2011.

9. Deebashree Mohanty, 'Braveheart Katara', The *Pioneer*, 8 March 2015.

10. 'Celebrating Women Who Fought the Much Needed Fight against Dowry', Sheroes.com, 29 June 2018.

11. Shreya Kalra, 'Dowry-Related Violence Kills Over 20 Women Daily', Feminisminindia.com, 12 March 2018. Even today, more than twenty women are killed every day in India for dowry, even as the laws women's rights activists Satya Rani Chadha and Shahjahan Apa fought for are being diluted.

12. From the profile by American artist Fazal Sheikh, 'Shahjahan Apa, Women's Rights Leader, Delhi, India, from the series Ladli', The Museum of Fine Arts, Houston, 2008, museum purchase funded by Jane P. Watkins.

13. Ibid.

14. T.V. Eachara Varier, *Memories of a Father*, translated from Malayalam by Neelan, Asian Human Rights Commission and Jananeethi, 2004.

15. Ibid.

16. Bobins Abraham, 'How a Determined Mother Fought for 13 Years to Get Justice for Her Son Killed in Police Custody', Indiatimes.com, 27 July 2018.

17. See the documentary Encountering Injustice: The Case of Meena Khalkho, produced by Women against Sexual Violence and State Repression, 2 March 2016, https://wssnet.org/2016/03/02/encountering-injustice-the-case-of-meena-khalko/#more-77073https://wssnet.org/2016/03/02/encountering-injustice-the-case-of-meena-khalko/#more-77073, accessed 9 June 2019.

18. Malini Subramaniam, 'Judicial panel confirms what a teenager's parents knew: police raped and killed their daughter', Scroll.in, 21 April 2015.

19. Ibid.

20. A procedure, since outlawed, where a rape victim's vaginal elasticity is tested by insertion of fingers, to pronounce on her sexual experience. See Jyotsna Singh's 'No two-finger test for rape', Down to Earth, 4 July 2015, https://www.downtoearth.org.in/news/no-twofinger-test-for-rape-40703, accessed 9 June 2019.

21. Tuka Ram and Others vs State of Maharashtra, on 15 September 1978, https://indiankanoon.org/doc/1092711/, accessed 9 June 2019.

22. We should also note here that Mathura was in love with a young man named Ashok, and her brother had filed a complaint with the police accusing Ashok and his family of kidnapping Mathura. The policemen had called in Mathura and Ashok and their family members to record their statements, and then detained Mathura and raped her. Mathura's story is often recollected as the story of how the law and courts tend to presume that if a woman has ever had consensual premarital sex, she is always available for sex with anyone. But Mathura's story also reminds us that parental or brotherly 'protection', which refuses to respect a woman's consensual sexual relationships, actually makes the woman more unsafe, more vulnerable to sexual violence.

23. 'The Newshour Debate: Apology or Arrogance?—Full Debate', YouTube, posted by Times Now, 9 December 2013, https://www.youtube.com/watch?v=zgFrc5UNkFs, minutes 19:3620:28. Also tweet by Subramanian Swamy, 'When I said Naxals believe in free sex I did not know Tejpal dictum: that modern secular girls will not object to sexual free enterprise', 18 January 2014, https://twitter.com/Swamy39/status/424755865023807488, accessed 9 June 2019. Also see

Swamy's tweet dated 29 October 2015, replying to Kavita Krishnan's tweet calling out an airline for barring a woman in a short skirt from a flight, by saying, 'These free sex Naxalites will defend passengers on flight wearing bikinis to rubbish "middle class" values', https://newsable.asianetnews.com/karnataka/here-is-the-truth-behind-gauri-lankeshs-free-sex-comment-and-subramanian-swamy-is-to-be-blamed-for-it, accessed 9 June 2019.

24. Ayesha Kidwai, 'Sanghis, Sex and University Students: What Is It Really All About?', Kafila, 28 April 2016, accessed 13 January 2019.

25. Dipankar Ghose, 'Chhattisgarh fake encounter: "I tell them all . . . my Meena was not Naxal"', *The Indian Express*, 19 July 2016.

26. Malini Subramaniam, 'By keeping minor girls in lockup at night, Chhattisgarh police breaks the law and triggers unrest', Scroll.in, 3 May 2015.

27. 'Bastar: Where the Constitution Stands Suspended', report by All India People's Forum based on a visit to Bastar in June 2016, http://aipf.online/2016/08/04/bastar-where-the-constitution-stands-suspended/, accessed 19 December 2019.

28. '*Bhagte hue naale mein giri do naksali, force ne kya dher*', *Bhaskar News Network*, 31 January 2016, http://www.bhaskar.com/news/CHH-OTH-MAT-latest-sukma-news-024004-3516841-NOR.html?seq=1, accessed 13 January 2019.

29. 'Bastar: Where the Constitution Stands Suspended', report by All India People's Forum based on a visit to Bastar in June 2016, http://aipf.online/2016/08/04/bastarwhere-the-constitution-stands-suspended/, accessed 19 December 2019.

30. Ibid.

31. Freny Manecksha, 'A Tribute to "The Mothers of Manipur"', review of Teresa Rehman's book *The Mothers of Manipur*, The Wire, 21 March 2017.

32. Krishnadas Rajagopal, 'Manorama "Mercilessly Tortured"', *The Hindu*, 13 June 2016.

33. '*Report of the Commission of the Judicial Inquiry (Manorama Death Inquiry Commission)*', 2004, https://hrln.org/wp-content/uploads/2018/07/report-of-commission-of-the-judicial-inquiry-manorama-death.pdf, accessed 9 June 2019.

34. Ibid.

35. Ibid.

36. Kavita Krishnan, 'Manipur Diary: A Report of the CPI(ML) Delegation's Visit to Manipur', *Liberation*, November 2004.

37. 'Buried Evidence: Unknown, Unmarked, and Mass Graves in Indian-administered Kashmir', International People's Tribunal on Human Rights and Justice in Indian-administered Kashmir, 2009.

38. Rifat Fareed, 'India ordered to probe 2,080 mass graves in Kashmir', Al Jazeera, 3 November 2017.

39. Uki Goñi, '40 years later, the mothers of Argentina's "disappeared" refuse to be silent', The *Guardian*, 28 April 2017.

40. Marcela Valente, 'Argentina: Remains of Mothers of Plaza de Mayo Identified', Inter Press Service News Agency, 8 July 2005.

41. Bryan Wawzenek, 'U2 Honors the "Mothers of the Disappeared"', https://diffuser.fm/u2-mothers-of-the-disappeared/, accessed 18 September 2019.

42. Pinochet unseated the democratically elected government headed by the Marxist president Salvador Allende in a US-backed coup in 1973 and ran a brutal dictatorship till 1990.

43. Sting, They Dance Alone, https://www.songfacts.com/facts/sting/they-dance-alone, last accessed 18 September 2019.

44. Eduardo Galeano, 'Dreams and Another Look at the Year 2000', English translation by Margaret Randall, *Z Magazine*, 1 December 1999.

45. 'Schoolgirls Throw Stones in Srinagar's Lal Chowk Earlier This Week,' photo credit: Nissar Ahmad, *The Hindu*, 29 April 2017.

46. Anuradha Bhasin Jamwal, 'Kashmiri Women as Stone Pelters: It Is Not Just Anti-Militarism, It's About Empowerment!', The Citizen, 27 April 2017.

47. Sanjay Kak, 'The Last Option: A Stone in Her Hand', The Times of India, 8 August 2010.

48. Essar Batool, Ifrah Butt, Munaza Rashid, Natasha Rather and Samreena Mushtaq, Do You Remember Kunan Poshpora (New Delhi: Zubaan Books, 2016).

49. 'Kunan Poshpora is a story not only of rape but of resistance', Natasha Rather speaking at the All India Progressive Women's Association conference in 2016, YouTube, 16 November 2016, https://www.youtube.com/watch?v=hRXxyOe-CE8, accessed 15 January 2019.

50. 'Why Are People Protesting in Kashmir? A Report', The Citizen, 11 May 2017.

51. 'Halla Bol: Debate Over Ramjas College Violence: Who Is Anti-National? Part 1', posted by Aaj Tak, YouTube, 27 February 2017, https://www.youtube.com/watch?v=eGVKIPOesZ8, accessed 12 June 2019.

52. Kavita Krishnan, 'When it Comes to Rape by Men in Uniform, the Media Forgets the Victim is Also Part of the "Nation"', The Wire, 26 April 2017.

53. 'Arnab Goswami, You Are the Most Unethical Journalist I Have Ever Seen: Kerala MP's Open Letter', Outlook, 30 May 2017.

54. Utkarsh Anand, 'Manipur: SC Calls for SIT to Probe Rape Charge against Soldiers', The Indian Express, 19 April 2017.

55. Anoo Bhuyan, 'Supreme Court Slams Claim That Manipur Fake Encounter Probe Will "Demoralise" Army', The Wire, 13 November 2018.

56. See for instance the Prime Minister's Independence Day speech in 2019, https://www.pib.nic.in/PressReleasePage.aspx?PRID=1582107, accessed 14 September, 2019.

57. 'Solidarity with the People of Kashmir: An Interview with Kavita Krishnan', Jacobin, https://jacobinmag.

com/2019/08/jammu-kashmir-narendra-modi-bjp-india-pakistan-article-370, accessed 15 September 2019.

58. '"Now We Can Bring Kashmiri Girls for Marriage": Haryana CM Khattar's Comment at Beti Bachao Event Leads to Controversy', *News 18*, 10 August 2019.

59. Piyush Srivastava, 'Marry fair Kashmiri girls, BJP MLA prods', *The Telegraph*, 8 August 2019.

60. Sheikh Saaliq, 'India's "patriotism pop" songs urge Hindus to claim Kashmir', Associated Press, 23 August 2019.

61. Aijaz Hussain, 'Kashmiris allege night terror by Indian troops in crackdown', Associated Press, 14 September 2019.

62. Barkha Dutt, 'How Indian and international journalists are missing the full story in Kashmir', *The Washington Post*, 10 September 2019

63. Ibid.

64. 'Pellet guns have killed 24, blinded 139 in Kashmir since 2010: Report', *Business Standard, 2* August 2019.

65. Joe Wallen, 'Kashmiri doctor arrested after warning blackout could cause deaths', *The Telegraph*, 27 August 2019.

Conclusion: Towards Fearless Freedom

1. John Romano, 'James Baldwin Writing and Talking', *The New York Times*, 23 September 1979.

2. Maheshwar, '*Srishti Beej Ka Naash Na Ho*', http://kavitakosh.org/kk/आज_लड़ाई_जारी_है_/_माहेश्वर, accessed 12 June 2019.

3. *The World Before Her*, written and directed by Nisha Pahuja, produced by Ed Barreveld, Cornelia Principe, Nisha Pahuja, edited by David Kazala, original music by Ken Myhr, Storyline Entertainment, Toronto, distributed by KinoSmith, 2012, www.worldbeforeher.com.

4. I owe this insight to Tanika Sarkar's oral observations about the film, in a private conversation.

5. Cinzia Arruzza, Tithi Bhattacharya and Nancy Fraser, *Feminism for the 99%: A Manifesto*, Verso, 2019.
6. Shuddhabrata Sengupta, 'Confronting the rules of rape', The *Caravan*, 1 February 2013.

Afterword

1. 'I'm scared, don't hang up: Hyderabad vet to her sister before being raped and murdered', India TV News, 29 November 2019.
2. Ibid.
3. Ibid.
4. Rakhi Bose, 'Hey Hyderabad Police, Instead of Advising Us on How Not to Get Raped, How About Telling Men Not to Rape', News18, 3 December 2019.
5. 'Calls for instant punishment to vet rape accused: Telangana', *Business Standard*, 5 December 2019.
6. 'Hyderabad vet murder: Trial will be conducted in fast-track court, says Telangana CM', Scroll.in, 1 December 2019.
7. '"Should Be Lynched", Says Jaya Bachchan As Telangana Vet Rape-Murder Case Rocks Parliament', *Outlook*, 2 December 2019.
8. Manisha Pande, 'Arnab Goswami's unhealthy obsessions peaked last night', Newslaundry, 13 July 2017.
9. 'TV Newsance Episode 70: ABP News and Aaj Tak's drama-reporting on Hyderabad rape case', Newslaundry, 7 December 2019.
10. 'Justice Served For Disha's Family | The Debate With Arnab Goswami', Republic TV, premiered on December 07, 2019, https://www.youtube.com/watch?v=uJvKT8kfOAw, last accessed December 13, 2019
11. Namrata Biji Ahuja, 'Active pursuit', *The Week*, 16 September 2018.
12. 'Arrested lawyer Sudha Bharadwaj says letter read out to media by police is "concocted"', Scroll.in, 1 September 2018.

13. 'Sudha Bharadwaj in jail for a year, police have found no evidence: Lawyer', *Business Standard*, 6 September 2019.
14. Kavita Krishnan, 'She speaks', Hardnews, 4 February 2013.
15. 'The Longest War', Rebecca Solnit, *Men Explain Things to Me: And Other Essays*, Haymarket Books, 2015.

ACKNOWLEDGEMENTS

For shaping my world and for sharing it, I want to thank:

My mother Lakshmi, and aunt Valli, the original roaming duo. We are lucky to have grown up with our imagination fired by the examples of adventurous and fearless girls. Thank you!

Nataraj and Ananthu, for love, laughter and every kind of support.

Thatha and Patti, Sharada Patti and Ananthanarayanan Thatha, Jyoti and Baba—you are missed.

Geeta-di, Jeeta, Ajanta, Srilata and Rama, who showed me the many ways of being a communist feminist.

I also want to thank:

Ma, for your unstinted love, and for the example of your quiet courage and independence.

Radhi, sister and friend, who walks the same path, frets more, laughs sweeter and lives kinder.

Om, for always being there to lean on, and for unfailing good cheer in all weather.

Vijay, for being part of the December 2012 movement, with your camera.

Heartfelt thanks to Amruta Patil, for generously allowing her Abhisarika Nayika for the cover artwork of this book.

Thank you, Kalpana Wilson, for two decades of friendship and productive Marxist feminist conversations.

S. Anand and Smita Patil, thank you for helping track down references for B.R. Ambedkar's writings.

Thank you, Revathi, for help with understanding Subramania Bharathi's poems.

Thank you, Toonika Guha and Manasi Subramaniam at Penguin Random House India, for suggesting I write this book. Both of you, together with Shreya Pandey, have given me all the support and confidence I needed along the way. Thanks to the entire team at Penguin Random House India for their patience with my many delays, and for making this book happen.

A heartfelt thank you to all the comrades of All India Students Association, All India Progressive Women's Association and the CPI(ML) over the past couple of decades—any strength, courage, insight, patience and empathy I have, I have learnt from you.

To all my many comrades in the women's movement, I want to say thank you for all that I have learnt from you, for being such staunch friends in need, and for the precious gift of critical solidarity.

Tapas—friend, comrade, companion, partner—you are the wind in my sails, thank you.